Will the Real God Please Stand Up

By Robin Moore Joyce

REJOYCE MOORE MINISTRIES

WILL THE REAL GOD PLEASE STAND UP
ISBN 978-0-9722577-2-5
Copyright © 2005 by Robin Moore Joyce
Rejoyce Moore Ministries, Inc.
428 Cokain Road
Harrisville, PA 16038
814-758-2263 or 814-786-9358
www.rejoycemoore.com

Printed in the U.S.A. by The Globe Printing Company, Inc.
129 West Neshannock Avenue
New Wilmington, PA 16142
800-995-7746

Dedication

Albert LaVerne Moore
June 17, 1928 to November 9, 2004

When I received Jesus Christ as my personal Savior and made Him Lord of my life, God soon revealed to me that He saves families. He guided me to several passages in the Bible that helped me to believe this promise for my own family.

One passage God used was Acts 16. Not once, but twice in Acts 16, we read of the salvation of households. The first was the salvation of Lydia and her household, and later, we read of the salvation of the Philippian jailer and his house. Throughout the Old and New Testament, we see the faithfulness of God to save families (Genesis 7:1; Joshua 6:25; John 4:53; Acts 10:24-48, 11:14, 18:7-8; Romans 16:10-11; 1 Corinthians 1:16, 16:15; 2 Timothy 4:19). And because God is not a respecter of persons, God immediately began the same work in my family.

Not long after my salvation, my niece and brother were saved. My brother and I seemed so hopelessly lost, yet we were so dramatically transformed through the life of Christ in us that it caused others in our family to take notice. My dad, Albert LaVerne Moore, was one of those who was most intrigued by our conversion.

In no way is this meant to dishonor or defame my dad, but he was often regarded as harsh, hard, uncaring, and at times, cruel. As with so many, life had dealt him some hard knocks that caused him to build up a hard exterior to protect himself. He was walled in so tightly no one was allowed in, and conversely, he was unable to get out of his self-made prison.

In my dad's eyes, God had become relegated to a religious form, and churches were filled with hypocrites. In so many ways, my dad was living a more moral life without God than many who claimed to know God. Not until he saw God dramatically change the lives of my brother and me, did he begin to hope for God to be more than what he had previously seen.

For the first time, my dad would listen as we spoke of our love for God and His ways. He saw miracle after miracle in his children's lives. But not until God ministered to him in a very personal way did his family began to see the prison walls my dad had built begin to crumble.

One Father's Day, while sitting in church, my pastor's wife asked me to say one good thing about my dad. I became ashamed and embarrassed because I was unable to think of one positive thing to say. Only then did I realize I needed God to heal my relationship with my dad. I began to pray that the Lord show me my dad through His eyes.

Soon God showed me the loving God-like qualities my dad had demonstrated as an excellent provider and a faithful, reliable father. He had been a rock of stability through out my troubled life. For years I had resented my dad for not giving me love the way I thought it should be, but I had ignored all the ways he did love me.

By the next Father's Day, I wrote a thank-you letter to my dad sharing with him all the ways God had shown me how my dad had loved me. God had healed me so completely through the power of forgiveness that I was overwhelmed with a great love for my dad. After my dad read my thank-you letter, he asked to speak with me. Since my dad had never made this request of me before, I was very apprehensive. With tears in his eyes, he thanked me for understanding how he loved his children. By the God-given ability to understand and accept my dad, it brought healing. And for possibly the second time in my life, my dad reached out and hugged me. We both found the love we needed. From that time on, the walls between my dad and I crumbled. I was able to pray prayers of thanksgiving for his salvation with assurance because now I could see him saved even before it was confirmed.

About two years after our relationship was healed, my dad was diagnosed with bladder cancer. At the same time, God had sent a new pastor to my church. He is a wonderful, spirit-filled man willing to take on seemingly impossible assignments. One of those assignments was my dad.

Due to the diagnosis, my dad had become despondent, and I invited my pastor to speak with him. They were both in their 70s and had a lot in common. After two hours of conversation and ministering the

Word of God, I heard my dad tell my pastor that he had already received the Lord as his Savior. And praise and glory to God, my dad even stretched his faith to believe for healing. By the end of that afternoon, he went from despondent to joy unspeakable. The Lord had done a mighty work.

From that moment on, I saw my dad become more open to God and more loving towards his family. His prison walls had been torn down. At the end of his life, his family had no doubt in their hearts and minds how much he loved them. And he had no doubt that his family loved him.

I credit my dad for helping me to experience Who God truly is. Therefore, I have dedicated this book, *Will the Real God Please Stand Up*, to him. Through my dad, God showed me what love is. God is love, and love is an action, not an emotion. God, as a loving Father, has already provided for us what we need when we need it because He is a faithful provider. Many people, based on emotions, believe that God should give them what they want when they want it. Others think God is holding out on them until they earn by works what He has for them. But only through a close personal relationship and fellowship with God, can we learn the truth. The truth is that we must trust Him at His Word. We must trust that He knows what we need when we need it. Through belief in Jesus Christ and His finished work on the cross, God has already made ample provisions for us that we can only attain by faith.

I am sharing my dad's story of salvation to give people hope. My dad seemed impossible to bring to salvation. But once God revealed Himself personally to my dad, he came.

God's promises are true. Let my dad's salvation be a testament to that truth. Only believe, and you will see the promises of God come to pass.

Table of Contents

Preface

This book is an effort to show the true nature and character of God. This may seem to be a lofty task, but I believe "all things are possible with God." God is pouring out His blessings upon us steadily, but our lack of understanding God's true nature and character keeps us from receiving from Him.

My desire is that believers will receive the message in this book so that they will live in the fullness of what God has for them. God wants His best for us. But rather than make God's best a daily goal, many in the body of Christ let their experiences (good or bad) dictate what they believe about God's will. If we are to be victorious, we must believe that God's Word is true and that His Spirit will train us in the ways of the Lord to obtain His best. Then, we will no longer let circumstances determine what we believe and what we do.

The Israelites are a great example of people who refused to believe God loved them and wanted His best for them. Therefore, at the end of each chapter, a section called *"Lessons from the Israelites"* has been included to help illustrate how the Israelites' lack of knowledge about God caused them to continually miss God's best. Scripture tells us,

> But with many of them God was not well pleased:
> for they were overthrown in the wilderness.

Now these things were our examples, to the
intent we should not lust after evil things, as
they also lusted.
Now all these things happen unto them for example: and they are written for our admonition,
upon whom the ends of the world are come.
(1 Corinthians 10:5, 6, and 11)

Through the examples of the Israelites, God has made it possible for us to learn from their mistakes. Please, take time to study the Israelites' experiences in order to avoid their many failures and subsequent pain and suffering.

Charles Henry Mackintosh's commentaries, *Notes on Exodus* and *Notes on Deuteronomy*, were used as primary resources for many of the *"Lessons from the Israelites."* Even though Mackintosh lived in the 1800s, his writings contain powerful revelations from God. What is most intriguing about his writings is his God-given ability to reveal God's unchanging love nature throughout the Old and New Testament.

A special thanks to Les Hodgett at STEM Publishing, 7 Primrose Way, Cliff's End, Ramsgate, CT125LF UK for helping to preserve and promote the writings of C. H. Mackintosh. The STEM Publishing website is <www.stempublishing.com. >. Many of Mackintosh's writings can be downloaded from The McBryan Family Online Books at the following website, <www.amcbryan.binternet.co.uk/docs.htm>.

Chapter One

God Is Love

And we have known and believed the love that God hath to us.
God is love;
and he that dwelleth in love dwelleth in God, and God in him.
1 John 4:16

Perfect Love

My opinion of God has changed dramatically over the years. I have gone from thinking of God as a mean, wrathful God (based on faulty Old Testament teaching as an impressionable child) to a God of love (according to the revelation knowledge of God's Word). I was so sure at the age of eighteen that God was out to get me that I excluded Him from my life until I was forty years old.

After receiving God's salvation by humbly asking Jesus into my heart, I began to see the love of God flowing to me and through me. God has shown me that love is the key to all the blessings in heaven. He told me that *"without the pursuit of perfect love, fear abounds, and faith drowns."* He has persuaded me that love is more powerful than any energy known to man. His love propels us into the supernatural realm. Perfect, sacrificial love makes the ordinary and common, extraordinary and uncommon. God's love enables us to resist giving people what they deserve and allows us to give them what they really want–love!

I am shameless when testifying about the wonderful love of God and what He has done for me. I have become alarmed, however, at how so many in the body of Christ believe that God is responsible for both good and evil. Many speak about God in a way that professes their belief that God haphazardly and arbitrarily causes blessings and curses. They credit God for both the good and the bad happenings in their lives. And usually the evil is chalked up to the "sovereign will of God" and/or the "tests and suffering they believed God uses to mold and shape them into His image."

Jesus Himself said:

> For God so loved the world, that he gave his
> only begotten son, that whosoever believeth in
> him should not perish, but have everlasting life.
> For God sent not his Son into the world to
> condemn the world; but that the world through
> him might be saved.
> (John 3:16-17)

This Scripture is filled with the promise of God's love and salvation, but often Christians ask, "How could a Father sacrifice a Son?" What they fail to see, due to unrenewed minds, is that God sacrificed Himself. Jesus tells us, "…Anyone who has seen Me has seen the Father.

How can you say then, Show us the Father? Do you not believe that I am in the Father, and that the Father is in Me? ..." (John 14:9-10 Amp).

The Father looked down upon His creation and sent Himself in the form of His Son to save us. That's how much He loves us. The love of God brought forth our Savior in the flesh of Jesus Christ. This demonstrated God's perfect love for us–to sacrifice Himself for His children.

God, our Father, wanted so much to have relationship and fellowship restored with His creation that He sacrificed His most precious Son. Yes, in worldly thinking, it makes God sound hard and cruel to sacrifice His Son. We must believe, however, that the Father and the Son are one with the same heart toward His children.

Think for a moment. What loving father on earth would not lay down his life for his children? The answer is not one. That should be our attitude concerning Jesus Christ laying down His life for the world. God gave Himself in the form of a child so that the requirement of the law would be fulfilled, and the redemption of the world would be available to all who believe in Him.

If John 3:16-17 is seen as both good and evil, it will cloud our ability to see God as love. Satan blinds us in such a way that we think we could love better than God, Who is love!

The Trinity

To help see the oneness of the Father and the Son, let us examine the three personalities of the Godhead.

And straightway coming up out of the water,
he saw the heavens opened, and the Spirit like
a dove descending upon him:
And there came a voice from heaven, *saying*,
Thou art my beloved Son, in whom I am well
pleased....
And there are three that bear record in heaven,
the Father, the Word, and the Holy Ghost, and
these three are one.
(Mark 1:10-11 and 1 John 5:7)

Here we see the three persons of the Godhead
manifested at the Jordan River: the voice of the Father, the
Word (Jesus) in a physical body, and the Holy Spirit like a
dove. Jesus came in the flesh to die for our sins. But before
He did, the Holy Spirit, Who came upon Him, anointed
Him for the work of the Father. None of this was possible,
however, without the Father's total acceptance and love
spoken in a blessing upon Jesus, "Thou art my beloved
Son, in whom I am well pleased." And this blessing of
His love and acceptance is for anyone who receives Jesus
Christ as his or her personal Savior.

Three distinct persons make up the Godhead. Yet,
"these three are one." I have always enjoyed the egg
analogy to help explain the three-in-one of the Trinity.
The egg has three distinct parts: the shell, the yoke, and
the white. While each part has its own name, purpose,
and function, they are one—an egg. And just like we
would not want a steady diet of the various parts of the

egg, we cannot have just one part of the Godhead. Error will most certainly be the outcome.

If we focus only on God the Father, we will see only His awesome, unattainable holiness mixed with His judgment without the hope of receiving God's grace and mercy. If we look only at Jesus, we will see God's grace and mercy without understanding God's holiness and judgment and why Jesus can be the only way to the Father. Finally, if we turn our attention to the Holy Spirit's awesome giftings of God's power, the power will be mishandled due to lack of God's wisdom and love.

The full picture of God can only be seen in the unity of the Trinity. Until we have the reality of Jesus Christ by the power of the Holy Spirit, we will never understand the Father and come into proper relationship and fellowship with Him. The three-in-one mystery of the Trinity is ever being revealed.

To Tell the Truth

To Tell the Truth was a popular TV show from the 1970s. The show consisted of a panel of celebrities asking three guests questions. The questions were designed to discover the true identity of one of the three guests. The other two guests were imposters. By the end of the show, the celebrities tried to sort out the truth from the lies and decided who were the imposters and who was not. The show always ended with a request: *Will the real _____ please stand up?*

My desire is that this book inspires you to start making the same request of God. *Will the real God please stand up?* Don't continue to rely on someone else's ideas, theories, and hunches about God. As you study, inquire of the Holy Spirit to show you the truth in God's Word so that your relationship and fellowship with God will grow. With this maturity will come the confidence to approach God in the knowledge that He has nothing but good and peaceful thoughts toward you. He only has plans to prosper you and to keep you safe from harm (See Jeremiah 29:11). The closer to the truth of God's love–the smaller the error one has concerning God's true nature and character.

Lessons from the Israelites:
The Trinity Revealed

Throughout God's dealings with the Israelites, God reveals His triune being. One such instance is in Exodus 17. The Israelites were thirsty and cried out to God, and God faithfully supplied their needs. What He did for them to satisfy their physical thirst is a type and shadow of what God has done for our spiritual thirst when we cry out to Him.

Moses was instructed to take his rod and strike the rock once. Then, out of the rock flowed a mighty river that satisfied millions. Spiritually speaking we are told, "They drank of that spiritual Rock that followed them: and that Rock was Christ" (1 Corinthians 10:4).

What we see in Exodus 17 is *God, our Holy Father*, revealing His requirement for holiness yet lovingly revealing how this requirement must be paid. Striking man could not pay the sin debt. Only striking Christ, the rock of our salvation, could pay that debt. Once the payment was completed, *the rock of our salvation, Christ*, was able to release *rivers of living water, the Holy Spirit*.

C. H. Mackintosh described the scene as follows:

> It was when the Rock of ages was cleft by the hand of Jehovah, that the flood-gates of eternal love were thrown wide open, and per-

ishing sinners invited by the testimony of the
Holy Ghost to "drink abundantly," drink deeply, drink freely. The gift of the Holy Ghost is the
result of the Son's accomplished work upon the
cross. "The promise of the Father" could not be
fulfilled until Christ had taken His seat at the
right hand of the majesty in the heavens, having
wrought out perfect righteousness, answered
all the claims of holiness, magnified the law
and made it honourable, borne the unmitigated
wrath of God against sin, exhausted the power
of death, and deprived the grave of its victory.[1]

In Exodus 17, God beautifully illustrates the role
of the Trinity in His redemptive plan for the world.
But in Exodus 33 and 34, we see the Trinity and the
redemptive plan of God revealed to just one person,
Moses. Moses only had to ask to see God's glory, and
God graciously agreed. God illustrated in a dramatic way
how personal and intimate salvation is intended to be for
each believer. Jesus died for the sins of the world, but,
more importantly, He died for each of us personally. God
wants us to experience His love and salvation so deeply
that we will in turn desire to become personally and
intimately involved with Him.

All of this may seem confusing since in Exodus 32,
God told Moses He would not go with Israel to the land
of promise because of their unbelief and rebellion. He
even said that He had the right to blot out the sinner

due to God's moral government. But Moses, who had experienced God's grace and mercy, asked to see the glory of God–the God of the gospel–that would blot out the sin but not the sinner.[2] Fortunately, for the Israelites, God agreed. The true character and nature of God was revealed to Moses and to us. God made all of His goodness pass before Moses.

> And he said, I beseech thee, show me thy glory.
> And he said, I will make all my goodness pass
> before thee, and I will proclaim the name of the
> LORD before thee; and will be gracious to whom
> I will be gracious, and will show mercy on
> whom I will show mercy.
> And he said, Thou canst not see my face: for
> there shall no man see me, and live.
> And the LORD said, Behold, *there is* a place by
> me, and thou shalt stand upon a rock:
> And it shall come to pass, while my glory passeth
> by, that I will put thee in a cleft of the rock, and
> will cover thee with my hand while I pass by:
> And I will take away mine hand, and thou shalt
> see my back parts: but my face shall not be seen.
> (Exodus 33:18-23)
>
> And the LORD passed by before him, and
> proclaimed, The LORD, The LORD God, merciful
> and gracious, longsuffering, and abundant in
> goodness and truth.

> Keeping mercy for thousands, forgiving
> iniquity and transgression and sin, and that
> will by no means clear *the guilty*; visiting the
> iniquity of the fathers upon the children, and
> upon the children's children, unto the third and
> to the fourth *generation*.
> (Exodus 34:6-7)

Now before Moses was able to look upon the glory of God, there were a few requirements. We are told that if Moses would stand on a rock close to God, God would safely place Moses into the cleft of the rock. Once Moses was properly placed in the rock, God covered Moses with His mighty hand of protection. Then, all of God's goodness passed by him. Before God's glory was seen, Moses heard God profess the name of the Lord and tell of His mercy, grace, longsuffering, goodness, truthfulness, forgiveness, and justice. Only after hearing God's Word could Moses see God's glory.

Please notice what Moses did *not* hear. He did *not* hear a condemning, harsh, wrathful God. The glory of God, as pictured in Exodus 33 and 34, is remarkably like Jesus. Jesus enables us to see God's true nature of love and goodness toward His creation. Jesus, the God of salvation, willingly suffered and died to pay the ransom for our deliverance from sin. Jesus, as the sin offering and scapegoat, met the requirement of a just and holy God so that our sin could be forgiven. Also, Jesus, as our resurrected Savior and Lord, made it possible for us to have an intimate relationship and close fellowship with a loving God.

I get chills when I see the total salvation picture in Exodus 33 and 34. Our requirement, as was Moses', is to stand on the rock of Jesus to partake in the salvation that God provided. And just as God placed Moses into the rock, so are we (by faith in Jesus and in the power of the Holy Spirit) placed into the body of Christ. And just as God covered Moses with His mighty hand, we are surrounded and filled with His Holy Spirit. God's loving touch of relationship and fellowship through Jesus and the Holy Spirit allows us to see His true nature of love and goodness. Once again we can see the presence of the entire Godhead.

Our intimacy with God causes us to desire Him as Lord of our lives. We will then desire to follow after him. Now, as followers of Jesus Christ, what part of God will we see? That's right, we will see His back. If we are looking at His face, it might mean we are out ahead of Him looking around bewildered. So, when God told Moses that he could not see God's face and live, this can be seen as our inability to live out ahead of God–out of His will. Remember, we are made as sheep to follow the shepherd.

Another interpretation that may explain the death upon looking at God's face involves true worship. True worshippers establish close fellowship with God as they sincerely seek God for Who He is and not what He can do. This requires dying to self. Thus, the only way to gaze upon the face of our God is to die to self-will and become like Jesus–a living sacrifice. When we receive the revelation of how much God loves us, we will love Him and desire what He desires.

Chapter Two

God Is Light

This then is the message which we have heard of him,
and declare unto you, that
God is light,
and in him is no darkness at all.
1 John 1:5

God's Will Be Done

Once someone told me that our suffering pleases
God and used the following Scripture as proof. "Yet
it pleased the LORD to bruise him; he hath put *him* to
grief: when thou shalt make his soul an offering for sin"
(Isaiah 53:10). This person explained that if God was
pleased to see His Son suffer for us, then our suffering
is just as pleasing to God. Because God had taught
me so much about His unconditional love, I could not
accept this as truth.

God is love. If a loving earthly father would not
take pleasure in his children's suffering, do we really
think God would be pleased with our suffering?

God was pleased, but the word "pleased" is used as
a function (will) not an emotion. "Pleased," as the world
understands it, relates to pleasure. But, in this case,
"pleased" refers to the final results of the sacrifice not the

sacrifice itself. The Amplified Bible states, "Yet it was **the will** of the Lord to bruise him."

Remembering that Jesus and the Father are One, read the prayer Jesus prayed in the Garden of Gethsemane. "…Father, if thou be willing, remove this cup from me: nevertheless not my will, but thine, be done" (Luke 22:42). What is the cup Jesus is referring to in this passage? Figuratively, the cup is defined as "one's lot or experience, whether joyous or adverse, divine appointments, whether favourable or unfavourable, are likened to a cup which God presents one to drink: so of prosperity and adversity."[1] Jesus was not praying to change the will of the Father (the final outcome of salvation for man); He was asking for another means by which to accomplish the Father's will.

The Bible tells us that Jesus was tempted in every way we are, yet He was without sin. Jesus' humanity is seen when He says, "…My soul is exceedingly sorrowful, even unto death…" (Matthew 26:38). Jesus' soul (mind, will, and emotions) was experiencing a sorrow deeper than any man can imagine, and we see the effect of this sorrow on His body in the Garden of Gethsemane. As He prayed, huge droplets of bloody sweat dripped off him. I believe that His sorrow was caused not so much by the foreseen physical pain He would endure, but by the thought of taking on the sins of the world that required being spiritually separated from the Father.

God's compassion (grace and mercy) is apparent, however, when we see God's answer to Jesus' prayer.

God's compassionate answer to Jesus was in the form
of an angel sent to strengthen Him. Read on further in
Matthew. We see Jesus coming out of the garden with a
renewed strength. Jesus, through prayer and supplication,
was enabled by God to complete the race set before Him.

Jesus never wavered. He was always in complete
agreement with the will of the Father. His prayers were
concerning the method in reaching the end result. He
and the Father are One, and Jesus, filled with sorrow,
knew that He would have to willingly be sacrificed and
be separated from the Father. No wonder He asked for
another way.

No one can imagine what Jesus had to endure at
the cross. Jesus (God himself) willingly placed himself
on the cross for us. Read on in Isaiah 53:10-11 (Amp).
Because of the work Jesus accomplished by going to
the cross and being raised from the dead, His spiritual
offspring have: prolonged life, prosperity, knowledge
of Him, and righteousness (right standing with God–
standing sinless and guiltless before the Father due to
the forgiveness of our sin).

So what pleased God? …the final result. Jesus,
who for the joy set before Him, endured the cross (See
Hebrews 12:2) and laid down His life in love for His
spiritual offspring (you and me). When we believe that
Christ died so that we are free from the bondage of sin
(the sin nature), then we enter into all that Christ did
for us. We are no longer to suffer from "sin, sickness/
disease, poverty, bad habits, lack of spiritual power, and

failure in prayer."[2] But we are born from above with all His inheritance. All the authority and power is in us and upon us to submit to God, resist the devil, and see the devil flee (See James 4:7). And what flees with the devil? All those things that steal, kill, and destroy. And what do we inherit through the redemptive life of Christ? We receive His life in outrageous abundance (See John 10:10)! It truly is Jesus plus nothing that equals everything!

Are Christians to Suffer?

Often I have been asked, "But doesn't it say in the Bible that we are to suffer for Jesus Christ's sake?" Well, let us examine this for a moment. Jesus (the Word, the Gospel, the Truth) Christ (the Anointed One and His Anointing) is Who we are to suffer for according to the Bible (See Philippians 1:27-30 and 2 Timothy 3:11-12). The Bible states clearly that when we preach Jesus Christ and the fullness of His grace to the world and the world's religious system, we are to be prepared to suffer. Suffer what?

> Persecution; reviling (contemptuous languages) and slander; false accusations; scourgings (whipping, punishing, afflicting); rejection by men; hatred by the world; hatred by relatives; martyrdoms; temptations; shame; imprisonments; tribulations; stonings; beatings; a spectacle to men; misunderstanding;

necessities, defamation, and despisings; trouble, affliction, distresses, tumults, labors, watchings, fastings, and evil reports; reproaches; trials; and satanic oppositions."[3]

Due to our religious freedom in America, we have not really experienced many of these sufferings just listed. Many Christians throughout the world, however, have suffered greatly even to the point of death just for confessing Jesus Christ as their Lord and Savior.

We live in a fallen world, and Satan is the god of this world. But, according to Hosea 4:6, God said that much of the suffering and destruction that many believers experience is due to lack of knowledge–lack of knowledge of God's Word (Jesus). Jesus suffered the same temptations that we suffer, yet He did so without sin. And sin is anything not of faith (See Romans 14:23). You see, as we become more knowledgeable of God's Word (Jesus), then God's faith (that we have all been given the same measure) sustains us. Doubt is replaced with steadfast belief. As we study His Word and allow the Holy Spirit to reveal His truths, we grow in Christ (the Anointed One and His Anointing). We allow Him to intercede for us; He becomes our wisdom and our strength. In Him we are set free from the bondages of sin, sickness, disease, and lack. "…The reason the Son of God appeared was to destroy the devil's works" (1 John 3:8 NIV). Jesus won the victory; therefore, Satan is a defeated foe. That explains why we are told to submit to God and to resist the devil. We are to enforce the victory that Jesus Christ won for us through His crucified body and resurrected life!

The Sovereignty of God

Many Christians use the sovereignty of God to excuse their unbelief. They claim that God wills, allows, and/or permits an evil (usually sickness or disease) to come upon them to teach them something. How this must break God's heart. The sovereignty of God, as it is taught today that nothing can happen except what God allows and/or that one can never know what God will do, is a lie. To teach the sovereignty of God this way is calling God a liar and keeping the body of Christ in bondage. Pretty strong words, but, please, keep reading.

God is sovereign–"supreme in power" (dominion); "superior to all others;" "supremely efficacious" (effectual); "superior in authority."[4] But God has chosen to set up His kingdom based on natural and spiritual laws that He will never violate. He has said in His Word, "My covenant will I not break or profane, nor alter the thing that is gone out of My lips" (Psalm 89:34 Amp).

For example, the law of sowing and reaping is both a natural and spiritual law. In the natural realm, a farmer sows seeds, and reaps a crop. If he sows corn, then he will reap corn. If he sows sparingly, then he will reap sparingly. In the spiritual realm, the law of sowing and reaping is the same. The type and amount of what one sows will determine the outcome of the harvest. Therefore, if we sow love abundantly, we will reap love abundantly.

God has limited Himself by His own words. We must believe that the Bible is the absolute truth and therefore, not subject to the changing moral and social climate of the world and its religious systems. The Bible is sometimes referred to as Basic Instructions Before Leaving Earth. As children of God, we have been born into God's kingdom, and as citizens, our duty is to learn the laws that govern His kingdom. When Christians do not study His Word, they can find themselves violating kingdom laws–not realizing that ignorance of the law does not exempt them from the negative consequences that result. In God's kingdom, just as in this world, we are responsible for living by the law of the land.

God is not a dictator in His kingdom; however, He gave us free will to decide for ourselves whether to choose life or death. We have the freedom to choose to accept Jesus as our Lord and Savior. We can choose to abide in Him, learn His ways, and do His will (following after kingdom laws). Or we can choose to live in the world and do according to the world's ways (violating kingdom laws). Ultimately, we choose life or death.

Knowing, understanding, and properly applying the truth of God's Word sets us free. Yet, *God will allow what we allow*. For example, I have had Christians argue their right to be sick because of the misguided thinking about the sovereignty of God. Their typical argument is, "If God wants me well, He will heal me." They mistakenly believe that God decides who gets healed and who does not. And some go so far as to say that God did not heal them because their sickness somehow glorifies Him. When all the while, God's Word assures believers that His will is to heal us (See Galatians 3:13 and Psalm 103:3). We have been set free from the "curse" of the Law through the shed blood and the resurrection of Jesus Christ. Read the curses in Deuteronomy 28 to see what we are free from *now* (See Appendix A: The Blessings and Curses of the Law). Do not let Satan steal, kill and destroy another day!

Please understand and believe that Jesus suffered the pain and humiliation of the cross and the separation from God, so we would not have to. Read Psalm 103 for encouragement and Romans for assurance.

Thank you, Jesus, for paying the price for our freedom from the sin nature and healing our spirit, soul, and body. John G. Lake refers to this as the "Triune Salvation."[5] If Adam died in three ways due to sin, our life through Christ is restored in three ways.

When Adam sinned against God, his spirit died (the life of God departed). He lost the intimate relationship he had with God. Adam's soul was quick to follow–letting "self" reign as god. He became aware of his nakedness (self-consciousness) and hid from God. Finally, Adam died physically at the age of 930. It took his body that long to learn how to die.

Jesus was the only One who could pay our sin debt in full so that we can live the abundant life He gave back to man. Immediately, upon believing and receiving Jesus as our Savior, our spirit is born from above, and we are made new creatures in Christ (See 2 Corinthians 5:17). As we make Jesus Lord of our lives, our soul (mind, will, and emotions) becomes like His. Finally, as a result of our renewed mind, we come to know the truth of God's Word for our physical health and wholeness. We will *not* permit sickness and disease to ravage our bodies. Instead, we will resist it. In Jesus we have been forgiven and healed. "Who forgiveth all thine iniquities; who healeth all thy diseases" (Psalm 103:3).

Often, upon hearing this, people will ask, "Yeah, but, how do you die? Isn't it appointed to everyone once to die?" Yes, people's bodies die, but why let Satan tell us how and when? As Christians, we are told to run the race set before us by fighting the good fight of faith, and when we are done, we can just fall asleep in the Lord.

Let us look at Jesus. Some may think that Satan told Jesus how and when to die, but don't believe that lie. Jesus chose to go to the cross in faith. Didn't He say He could have commanded legions of angels to fight for Him? Also, Jesus tells us, "Therefore doth my Father love me, because I lay down my life, that I may take it again" (John 10:17). And when Jesus understood that His race was over He said, "It is finished" and committed His spirit to the Father. Does this sound like Satan had any control in how and when Jesus died? No. Scripture tells us if they had known God's plan, "…they would not have crucified the Lord of glory" (1 Corinthians 2:8).

Let's rejoice in the knowledge, understanding, and wisdom of God's Word as the Holy Spirit teaches us. Then we can boldly go out and with confidence confess the "Good News" to the world–remembering that the only suffering that Jesus Christ has told us to endure is for the Gospel's sake.

The Tests and Sufferings of Evil

The tests of evil that come as a result of living in a fallen world have been overcome by the blood of Jesus and in the power of His resurrection. We overcome by the blood of the lamb and the Word of our testimony (See Revelation 12:11). We are overcomers and an occupying army for God until Jesus returns. The only time these tests cause unbearable suffering is when we are not prepared for the test. The renewing of the mind through the Word of God prepares us. It may look bleak at times, but we can trust that the Word of God will resurrect those dead things in our lives. Scripture says God is the One Who gives life to dead things, and He is the One Who calls things that are not as if they are (See Romans 4:17).

Death may be staring us right in the face, but we are told to resist the devil and submit to what the Lord has to say about it. We are to reject Satan's lies and say what God says. If we are sick, we are to say, "By His stripes I am healed." As our mind and mouth line up with our born again spirit, we will see the devil flee (See James 4:7).

The testing of our faith causes unbearable suffering only when we are not prepared. In the natural, a test is only painful and distressing when we are not fully persuaded through preparation (study). A test is not unbearable if we are completely confident that we have studied the right material and have meditated on it to the point that it just flows from us unobstructed. We cannot be shaken by what we see because we are fully persuaded that we know the answers.

Spiritually, we must do the same. The Bible is full of God's answers to meet any need, any circumstance, and any crisis. But the Bible cannot help us if we never study it. Scripture tells us:

> Every Scripture is God-breathed (given by His inspiration) and profitable for instruction, for reproof *and* conviction of sin, for correction of error *and* discipline in obedience, [and] for training in righteousness (in holy living, in conformity to God's will in thought, purpose, and action),
> So that the man of God may be complete *and* proficient, well fitted *and* thoroughly equipped for every good work.
> (2 Timothy 3:16-17 Amp)

Often, I have heard Christians say that God causes or allows the evil tests of this world to come into our lives to accomplish the same purpose as the Word. This is most certainly inaccurate. God tells us just the opposite.

Blessed (happy, to be envied) is the man who
is patient under trial *and* stands up under
temptation, for when he has stood the test *and*
been approved, he will receive [the victor's]
crown of life which God has promised to those
who love Him.
Let no one say when he is tempted, I am
tempted from God; for God is incapable of being tempted by [what is] evil and He Himself
tempts no one.
But every person is tempted when he is drawn
away, enticed *and* baited by his own evil desire
(lust, passions).
Then the evil desire, when it has conceived,
gives birth to sin, and sin, when it is fully ma-
tured, brings forth death.
Do not be misled, my beloved brethren.
Every good gift and every perfect (free, large,
full) gift is from above; it comes down from
the Father of all [that gives] light, in [the shining of] Whom there can be no variation [ris-
ing or setting] or shadow cast by His turning
[as in an eclipse].
(James 1:12-17 Amp)

Clearly, God is saying He does not bring evil upon
us. No! Evil comes into our lives by Satan's doing, our
doing, or the result of living in a fallen world. If evil
does come, however, the test does not have to cause us

fear. If we allow the fruit of patience to work (sustaining our faith over a period of time; remaining unchanged or immovable by the circumstance) by standing on the Word in faith (fully persuaded), we will receive what God has already called ours–the victory in Christ Jesus. As we allow God's mercy and grace to operate in our lives and resist the devil, we will see what Satan meant for destruction turned into good (See Genesis 50:20; Romans 8:28). We are told to rejoice, not at the circumstance, but at the expectant hope and faith in God's promise of deliverance from all evil.

God's deepest desire is for His children to be trained by His Word. "So then faith *cometh* by hearing, and hearing by the word of God" (Romans 10:17). Faith does not come from Satan's mischief. Please, begin to study God's Word for yourself. Do not allow years of wrong teaching, half-truths, and lies keep you in bondage one more day. Let the truth of God's Word (the knowledge, understanding, and wisdom of Jesus) set you free. Let Jesus be the Savior and the Lord of your life, and you will allow God's blessings to be poured out from heaven.

Lessons from the Israelites: "All That the Lord Hath Spoken We Will Do" VS "Be It unto Me According to Thy Word"

For years reading Exodus would make me very confused about God especially in the way He dealt with the Israelites before, during, and after Exodus 19. But confusion turned to understanding after reading C. H. Mackintosh's *Notes on Exodus*.

Before Exodus 19, the Israelites doubted constantly God's goodness and ability. But God continued to extend His grace by blessing them with deliverance, health, wealth, food, water, guidance, and protection. Even when they murmured, God told them to come near to Him and behold His glory (See Exodus 16:9-10). He was encouraging them to trust Him for He was their only necessity.

Even at the beginning of chapter 19, God lovingly expressed His ultimate desires for the children of Israel.

> Ye have seen what I did unto the Egyptians, and *how* I bare you on eagles' wings, and brought you unto myself.
> Now therefore, if ye will obey my voice indeed, and keep my covenant, then ye shall be a peculiar treasure unto me above all people: for all the earth *is* mine:
> And ye shall be unto me a kingdom of priests,

and an holy nation. These *are* the words which
thou shalt speak unto the children of Israel.
(Exodus 19:4-6)

And how did the people respond to God's words of
invitation and love? Scripture says, "…And all the people
answered together, and said, All that the LORD hath
spoken we will do…" (Exodus 19:8).

When I read their response, I thought that would
make God pleased. But note God's reaction. When God
came down to Mount Sinai, He instructed Moses to set up
boundaries around the mount. He also imposed the death
penalty for anyone that crossed that boundary. Then God
instituted another covenant, the law of works, filled with
do's and don'ts and earned blessings or curses.

Now, I don't know if that sounds confusing to you,
but, personally, I thought God was being moody. He had
told the people that if they obeyed His voice and kept His
covenant, He would bless them. The children of Israel
would be His peculiar treasure, His kingdom of priests,
and His holy nation. But once they said, "we will do,"
God appears to get cranky.

Mackintosh writes that those three little words, *"we
will do,"* are responsible.

This was bold language. They did not
even say, "we hope to do" or "we will endeavor
to do." This would have expressed a measure of
self-distrust. But no; they took the most abso-

lute ground. "We will do." Nor was this the
language of a few vain, self-confident spirits
who presumed to single themselves out from
the whole congregation. No; "all the people answered together." They were unanimous in the
abandonment of the "holy promise"–the "holy
covenant." ...In a spirit of dark and senseless
legality, [they] abandoned Jehovah's covenant
of pure grace for man's covenant of works.[6]

Mackintosh points out that early in chapter 19, God
was referring to the Abrahamic covenant, and He was trying
to confirm that same covenant in Abraham's descendents,
the Israelites. By obedience to His Word and by faith in
His covenant to Abraham, they were being invited into the
abundant blessings of God's grace. He writes,

What was the utterance of that "voice?"
and what did that "covenant" involve? Had Jehovah's voice made itself heard for the purpose
of laying down the rules and regulations of a
severe and unbending lawgiver? By no means.
It had spoken to demand freedom for the captivity, provide a refuge from the sword of the
destroyer–to make a way for the ransomed to
pass over–to bring down bread from heaven, to
draw forth water out of the flinty rock....
And as to His "covenant," it was one of
unmingled grace. It proposed no conditions–it

made no demands–it put no yoke on the neck–
no burden on the shoulder. When "the God of
glory appeared unto Abraham," in Ur of the
Chaldees, He certainly did not address him in
such words as, "thou [s]halt do this," and "thou
shalt not do that." Ah! [N]o; such language was
not according to the heart of God.... His word
to Abraham was, "I WILL GIVE."[7]

Mackintosh makes clear what changed God's
approach in dealing with the children of Israel.

> The moment Israel uttered their "singu-
> lar vow," the moment they undertook to "do,"
> there was a total alteration in the aspect of
> things.... The sweet accents of grace and mercy
> are exchanged for the "thunderings and light-
> nings" of the fiery mount. Man had presumed
> to talk of his miserable doings in the presence
> of God's magnificent grace. Israel had said, "we
> will do," and they must be put at a distance in
> order that it may be fully seen what they are
> able to do. God takes the place of moral dis-
> tance; and the people are but too well disposed
> to have it so, for they are filled with fear and
> trembling; and no marvel, for the sight was
> "terrible,"–"so terrible that Moses said, I ex-
> ceedingly fear and quake." Who could endure
> the sight of that "devouring fire," which was

the apt expression of divine holiness?… "Our
God is a consuming fire,"–perfectly intolerant
of evil, in thought, word, and deed.[8]

Mackintosh points out that the hardness of the
Israelites' hearts through unbelief and self-righteousness
ushered in God's perfect moral law to prove to the
children of Israel how lacking they were to "do"
anything. And for the next 2,000 years, the Israelites
proved over and over their inability to keep the law of
works. "Law sets forth what man ought to be; grace
exhibits what God is."[9]

Mackintosh is quick to clear up any confusion that
may be caused by a passage in Deuteronomy that says,

And the LORD heard the voice of your words,
when ye spake unto me; and the LORD said unto
me, I have heard the voice of the words of this
people, which they have spoken unto thee: **they
have well said all that they have spoken.**
(Deuteronomy 5:28, *emphasis mine*)

Please read Deuteronomy 5 in its entirety. One can
see that Moses was recounting events that occurred after
the Israelites boldly spoke the words, "we will do," in
Exodus 19. Moses was retelling events from Exodus 20.

In Exodus 20, God had spoken His Ten
Commandments directly to His people. They
immediately shrank back in terror and asked that Moses

speak to them rather than God. They feared that if God spoke to them any longer, they would die.

Their reaction was a direct result of the Law. The Law makes men aware of their inability to meet God's holy standard, and thereby makes them desperate for a mediator to bridge the gap between God and themselves. When Moses quoted God saying, "They have well said all that they have spoken," Moses was referring to the scene in Exodus 20 when the Israelites recognized their need for a mediator.

But God did not tell the Israelites they had spoken well in Exodus 19 when they said, "We will do." How should the Israelites have responded to God? What would have allowed them to continue in grace? For the possible answers to these questions, let us examine the sharp contrast between the Israelites' response and the Virgin Mary's response to God's will.

The angel Gabriel had told Mary, who had never been with a man, that she would have a baby. She did ask for more details to clear up some confusion but then responded in faith, "Be it unto me according to thy word" (See Luke 1:38).

The Israelites' bold words, "We will do," eventually made them stand afar off from God. But Mary's humble, faith-filled words, "Be it unto me according to thy word," made her pregnant with God's Word.

In the natural, pregnancy requires intimacy, and the same is true in the spiritual realm. For one who comes to know God intimately through Jesus Christ, a pregnancy occurs that gives birth to a new life in Christ. As one grows in Christ, one will continually conceive and give birth as the plans and purposes of God become manifested in the life of a believer.

Notice that without the work of the Holy Spirit, Mary would never have conceived. The same is true for believers. The Holy Spirit draws us to Jesus in order to receive salvation. Once we are saved, the Holy Spirit guides and teaches us by the Word. Without the indwelling power of the Word and Spirit of God, we cannot complete the work that God has hand picked us to do. Therefore, without having both Jesus (the Word) and Christ (the Anointed One and His Anointing), we will not come into the close fellowship and intimacy that causes the Word to become manifested in this world.

We are to be as Mary, by saying to God in faith, "Be it unto me, according to thy word," so that the Word can become flesh. Stop saying those faithless words, "If it be thy will," and get to know what God's will is. Once we know His will by studying His Word through the power of His Spirit, we will humbly but confidently speak what Mary spoke. We will become pregnant with the promises of God for ourselves, our families, our neighborhoods, our country, and our world. As we seek God because He has become our dearly beloved Father, we will see the Lord's life lived in us and through us.

"We will do" makes us lord and god of our lives. "Be it unto me, according to thy word," however, causes us to allow God to be Lord of our lives. We can trust that by grace He will make us His peculiar treasure, His kingdom of priests, and His holy nation.

God Is a Spirit

God is a Spirit:
and they that worship him must worship him in spirit and in truth.
John 4:24

The Holy Spirit

In the previous chapter, we have seen the vital importance of the Word of God. God's Word can only be understood, however, through the revelation of God's Spirit. Without the Holy Spirit to lead and guide us into all truth, the reading of His Word is only a mental exercise. One cannot have the seed of God's Word germinate and grow into a mature, life-altering fruit without the fertilizating and watering by the Holy Spirit. Jesus tells us:

> But the Comforter (Counselor, Helper, Intercessor, Advocate, Strengthener, Standby), **the Holy Spirit**, Whom the Father will send in My name [in My place, to represent Me and act on My behalf], **He will teach you all things**. And He will cause you to recall (will remind you of, bring to

your remembrance) everything I have told you.
(John 14:26 Amp, *emphasis mine*)

There are times when we read God's Word that it does not minister to us at all. But when we allow the Holy Spirit to teach us the truths hidden in His Word, the Word becomes permanently planted in our heart through understanding and grows out of our heart through the practical application of it (wisdom). God's Word goes from seed to fully developed fruit for sustaining life. This growth process of God's Word is due to the power of the Holy Spirit.

Scripture also tells us not only to hear the Word of God but also to be a doer of His Word (See James 1:22). To be a doer of the Word as God wills, however, we must trust and rely on His Spirit for the proper direction and guidance. Only God by His Spirit can show us the good works He has for us to do. We are told,

For no other foundation can anyone lay than that which is [already] laid, which is Jesus Christ (the Messiah, the Anointed One).
But if anyone builds upon the Foundation, whether it be with gold, silver, precious stones, wood, hay, straw.
The work of each [one] will become [plainly, openly] known (shown for what it is); for the day [of Christ] will disclose *and* declare it, because it will be revealed with fire, and the fire

will test and critically appraise the character *and*
worth of the work each person has done.
If the work which any person has built on this
Foundation [any product of his efforts what-
ever] survives [this test], he will get his reward.
But if any person's work is burned up [under
the test], he will suffer the lose [of it all, losing
his reward], though he himself will be saved,
but only as [one who has passed] through fire.
(1 Corinthians 3:11-15 Amp)

So, if we are allowing God's Word and His Spirit
first place in our lives, we will see more treasure than not.
We will hear, "Well done, My good and faithful servant."

Believers must understand that only the proper
application of His Word by faith is the work (the
treasures) stored up in the kingdom of God. We can do
many things that look godly, but without the leading and
guiding of the Holy Spirit, our works are the dead works
burned up as chaff. So, reading and studying God's Word
is not enough. God's Word through the inspiration of the
Holy Spirit must lead us.

Tests of Obedience and Motive

Let us revisit the notion of tests and suffering, but
this time let us examine what God's tests are. They are
tests (putting to proof)[1] through **obedience** and tests
(putting to proof) of **motives**. God tests our obedience to

His Word forcing us to examine our faith and belief in it. Also, He tests our motives behind our obedience causing us to examine why we are serving Him. His Spirit is constantly with us to remind us that love must always be our motive for honoring God's Word.

Scripture says,

> I APPEAL to you therefore, brethren, *and* beg of you in view of [all] the mercies of God, to make a decisive dedication of your bodies [presenting all your members and faculties] as a living sacrifice, holy (devoted, consecrated) and well pleasing to God, which is your reasonable (rational, intelligent) service *and* spiritual worship.
>
> Do not be conformed to this world (this age), [fashioned after and adapted to its external, superficial customs], but be transformed (changed) by the [entire] renewal of your mind [by its new ideals and its new attitude], so that you may prove [for yourselves] what is the good and acceptable and perfect will of God, *even* the thing which is good and acceptable and perfect [in His sight for you].
>
> God is a Spirit (a spiritual Being) and those who worship Him must worship *Him* **in spirit** and **in truth** (reality).
>
> (Romans 12:1-2 & John 4:24 Amp, *emphasis mine*)

As God has ministered to me over the years by His Word and by His Spirit, He has asked me to do things that have required selflessness on my part. Remembering that a test only causes suffering when you are not prepared, I can tell you initially these tests caused me pain. Offering up your body as a living sacrifice (dying to self) can be painful. As I studied God's Word by inspiration of His Spirit, however, my thinking has begun to line up more with His. The renewal of my mind has caused my desires and my behavior to be more like Christ's.

The first time I realized my thinking and reacting had changed was after God required me to do a selfless act. I had an unavoidable relationship with someone that had become a source of bitterness for me. I wanted to cut off all ties with her, which was my approach to most hurtful relationships before I made Jesus Christ my Savior and my Lord. God's ways, however, are about love and forgiveness. So, one day after being hurt once again by this person, I began to rant about her treatment of me. Then I heard the still small voice of the Holy Spirit urging me to bless her. What my flesh said was no! But what my reborn again spirit and renewed mind said was yes!

So I had a decision to make. Do I allow my flesh (my carnal mind) to dominate? Or do I let the new life in Christ (my spirit) rule over these circumstances? With gritted teeth I got in agreement with God. As soon as I made that decision for Christ to bless that person, a peace and calm washed over me. I no longer felt bitter and angry. I was freed from all the awful emotions. I cried tears of joy and started to praise God. I was then able to bless that person not expecting anything in return. I did not care about any reward for doing the good work of God because I already was rewarded with the wonderful feeling of love that replaced the anger.

What part of that test was God, and what part was Satan, the flesh, or living in a fallen world? The person who had been a "thorn in my side" for months was just allowing her "flesh" to continue to dominate her. God was not testing me by using this person in order to teach me something. God does not test with evil; Satan is the one who tempts with evil (See James 1:13).

God's test was the test of obedience–asking me to choose life and not death. He used that test to purify my soul (my mind, will, and emotions). The test was not showing God anything new. He knew my heart, and He already knew the way I would respond. No, the test was to show me how much of His Word I believed and would act upon. I could not have done it without His Spirit encouraging me and strengthening me. By passing that test, I now know the great reward of peace of mind that forgiveness and blessing others through God's love brings. I am now fully persuaded that by allowing God's forgiveness and love to have their perfect work, God's tests do not bring suffering. The more I become acquainted with Him through His Word and His Spirit, the more I know that His tests are fair and good. They become easier to pass as I spend time with Him in preparation for those tests.

God also uses similar tests to reveal His children's motives. We can do things that appear godly yet do them with wrong motives. For instance, one day while I was studying His Word, the Holy Spirit questioned my motives. Now, what could be wrong with studying His Word? What was wrong was my motive.

In the course of a week, various people had confronted me in two different Bible studies about my understanding of various Scriptures in God's Word. Please pay careful attention to the words that I use to describe my attitude. Of course, I "argued" my position. Then I became "offended," especially after hearing that those who "attacked" me rarely spent time studying God's Word. Then I began to search the Word for the "ammunition" I needed to shore up my "argument."

Immediately, the Holy Spirit addressed me concerning what I was doing. First, He asked me why I was studying His Word. In "pride" I used 2 Timothy to explain that God has commanded me to do so to show myself approved.

> Study *and* be eager *and* do your utmost to present yourself to God approved (test by trial), a workman who has no cause to be ashamed, correctly analyzing *and* accurately dividing [rightly handling and skillfully teaching] the Word of Truth. (2 Timothy 2:15 Amp)

Without hesitation, He instructed me to read on in 2 Timothy.

> And the servant of the Lord must not be quarrelsome (fighting and contending). Instead, he must be kindly to everyone *and* mild-tempered [preserving the bond of peace]; he must be a skilled *and* suitable teacher, patient *and* forbearing *and* willing to suffer wrong.
> He must correct his opponents with courtesy *and* gentleness, in the hope that God may grant that they will repent and come to know the Truth [that they will perceive and recognize and become accurately acquainted with and acknowledge it].
> (2 Timothy 2:24-25 Amp)

What God, by His Spirit and His Word, was able to show me was my wrong motive. He was testing my motives by asking me that simple question: Why are you reading My Word? On the surface, it seemed like an odd question since we are told by Him to do so. But He sees the heart of man and their motives for doing every seemingly good work. By this test, He showed me that my motive was wrong. The purifying of His children comes from testing their good deeds, so we can guard our hearts.

How often do we do good deeds because we are afraid of what others might say if we do not? "Fear of man" and "to be seen of men" are wrong motives for doing good works and is the stubble that will be burned (See 1 Corinthians 3:11-15). Only through the teaching, leading, and guiding of the Holy Spirit can we do the works that the Father has for us to do. For He is the only One Who has the good, acceptable, and perfect plan for our lives (See Romans 12:2).

True Worship

When we allow His Word and His Spirit to have their way in our lives, we become the true worshippers spoken of in John 4:24. True worshippers worship in the spirit. They become totally dependent on God's Spirit for the strength to allow God to do His will through them. True worshippers worship also in the truth. They are more concerned about the truth and reality of God than the formality of religion and the traditions of man. True worshippers will desire what God desires. I now understand King David's passionate plea, "Create in me a clean heart, O God; and renew a right spirit within me" (Psalm 51:10).

As a believer, I understand that my spirit is 100% saved. My spirit is perfect–reborn with the fullness of the life of Christ. I understand, however, that while I am on this earth, my soul (my mind, will, and emotions) is being saved. The salvation of my spirit only becomes manifested in my soul through His Word and His Spirit. Therefore, this is my prayer. Lord, I want to be a true worshipper. Like David, I give you permission to purify me (cleanse my mind, will, and emotions) with your tests of obedience and of motives so that my heart does not become hard and less responsive to Your Word and Your Spirit.

I pray the following prayer from Ephesians every day to help keep my heart sensitive to God. I have made it more personal by changing the pronouns.

> That the God of our Lord Jesus Christ,
> the Father of glory, may give unto (me)
> the spirit of wisdom and revelation in the
> knowledge of him:
> The eyes of (my) understanding being enlight-
> ened; that (I) may know what is the hope of his
> calling, and what are the riches of the glory of
> his inheritance in the saints,
> And what *is* the exceeding greatness of his
> power to (me) who believes, according to the
> working of his mighty power.
> (Ephesians 1:17-19)

God's wisdom (proper application of God's Word) keeps us in true worship. James has explained this better than I can. Throughout his writings, He exalts the wisdom of God. First, he tells us to ask for wisdom if we are deficient in it, and God will give it liberally (See James 1:5). Later, he explains what that wisdom is and what it does for a believer.

But the wisdom from above is first of all pure
(undefiled); then it is peace-loving, courteous
(considerate, gentle). [It is willing to] yield to
reason, full of compassion and good fruits; it
is wholehearted *and* straightforward, impartial
and unfeigned (free from doubts, wavering,
and insincerity).
And the harvest of righteousness (of conformity to God's will in thought and deed) is
[the fruit of the seed] sown in peace by those
who work for *and* make peace [in themselves
and in others, that peace which means con-
cord, agreement, and harmony between individuals, with undisturbedness, in a peaceful
mind free from fears and agitating passions
and moral conflicts].
(James 3:17-18 Amp)

Finally, we can see the ultimate outcome as we
become more submitted to God's ways. "Humble
yourselves [feeling very insignificant] in the presence
of the Lord, and He will exalt you [He will lift you up
and make your lives significant]" (James 4:10 Amp).
We see by these passages from James that by getting
into agreement with God according to His Word and
His Spirit we are truly worshipping God in Spirit and
in Truth. As we read His Word through the revelation
knowledge, understanding, and wisdom of God's Spirit,
we will see first, our thoughts, next, our mouth, then, our

actions transformed into the likeness of Jesus Christ. Our obedience will slowly involve less pain, and our motives will be according to what God wills for us.

Just as growth in the natural is a process so is spiritual growth. The transformation from a carnal Christian (one still led by the unrenewed mind, will, and emotions) to a spirit-led Christian is a process. Jesus explained this process in a parable. Jesus assures us that the seed that we plant (the Word that we plant and allow the Holy Spirit to fertilize and water) will grow. The process will be "...first the blade, then the ear, after that the full corn in the ear" (Mark 4:28).

As we learn more about God, we begin to trust Him more. We trust that He is leading and guiding us into all truth by His Spirit. We believe that He has a good plan for us–a plan of good and not of evil (See Jeremiah 29:11). We become well prepared for His tests of obedience and motives–passing them with ease. We do His will with love, joy, peace, patience, kindness, goodness, faithfulness, gentleness, and self-control because we have confidence in Him. We have confidence that He is able to complete His work in us and through us. In a little while, we begin to see ourselves as His peculiar treasure and His glory here on earth. All the while we are storing up treasures in heaven that cannot be burned away by God's purifying fire.

Lessons from the Israelites: Pharaoh's Counterfeit Worship

Let us compare the worship (service, lifestyle) that God wanted from the people of Israel (God's people) to the worship that Egypt (the world) and Pharaoh (the devil) offered. God wanted His people completely delivered and separated from Egypt so that His people could worship Him, as He desired. Pharaoh, however, had four variations of worship he was pressuring God's people to accept.

Pharaoh proposed to Moses and Aaron his first form of worship. "Go, sacrifice to your God here in the land" (Exodus 8:25 NIV, *emphasis mine***).**

C. H. Mackintosh points out that this worship on the common ground of Egypt would have put God (Jehovah) on the same level as their gods. They could then say no difference existed between Israel's worship of Jehovah and their worship of the gods of Egypt.[2]

We see this very clearly in today's society. The world realizes a need for something greater than themselves and accepts the possibility of a God, an energy, etc. Many even agree that having some form of religion is good and will accept a worldly religion. But the world does not desire a God that is real or a God that has substance in the form of Jesus Christ (our Lord and Savior–the name above all names). They do not desire a loving, caring God

Who wants to have a personal relationship with them because then they become responsible for their part in that intimate relationship.

No, Satan would rather we never know the one true God through Jesus Christ. Satan wants us to keep God far off in a distant land. Satan's desire is that we stay in the world and create a god in our own image (a human religion). But God has called us out of the world to worship Him in spirit and in truth.

Pharaoh's second form of worship was this. "Pharaoh said, I will let you go to offer sacrifices to the Lord your God in the desert, but you must not go very far" (Exodus 8:28 NIV, *emphasis mine*).

In this form of worship, Mackintosh observes that if Pharaoh could not keep them in Egypt to worship, he would keep them very near. This would make it easier for the Israelites to return to Egypt if things got difficult.[3]

Again, we can see the application for today. How often have we seen people make a profession of faith in Christ and try in their own power to live for Him, only to give up and run back to the world. This has a devastating effect especially on unbelievers who are watching Christians. Those people, who appear to separate themselves unto Christ and then reject Him to return to the world, cause confusion. They help support scoffers' arguments against Christ's ability to transform lives. What an unbeliever cannot spiritually discern is that discipling believers is vital so that their hearts and minds become aligned with the Word of God. Once we see the kingdom of God as our new home, going back to the world becomes unimaginable.

Pharaoh made known to Moses and Aaron his third counterfeit worship. "Pharaoh said, The LORD be with you–if I let you go, along with your women and children! Clearly you are bent on evil. No! Have only the men go; and worship the LORD, since that's what you have been asking for" (Exodus 10:10-11 NIV, *emphasis mine*).

Mackintosh shows how Pharaoh's third form of worship would only partially deliver the Israelites. Without their entire families, the Israelites would not have left the land of Egypt. Their hearts would have been held captive (distracted by worry) for their family members still held in Egypt.[4]

Christian families are the same today. How many Christian parents are held captive by Satan because their children are living in the world? Parents allow their minds to become captured by thoughts of worry and fear for their children and stop God from doing His will in their families. Yet God has given His Word that if we "Train up a child in the way he should go: and when he is old, he will not depart from it" (Proverbs 22:6). We can trust God for the salvation of our children.

Some parents may say, "But I didn't raise my children up in the way of the Lord." Well, God has another promise for us.

> But the mercy of the LORD *is* from everlasting
> to everlasting upon them that fear him, and his

> righteousness unto children's children;
> To such as keep his covenant, and to those that
> remember his commandments to do them.
> (Psalm 103:17-18)

Here we see that those who are saved, even after their children are raised, can depend on God to save their children and grandchildren. We see this in Acts 16 that not only the jailer was saved, but also his entire family was saved. I believe that our faith-filled, compassionate prayers for our families allow God's angels to go to work guiding and directing laborers to harvest our families.

I saw this first in the Bible and now in my own family. God saves families. No, God does not override free will, but through prayers of binding the spirit of blindness (See 2 Corinthians 4:4) and loosing laborers (See Matthew 9:38), we will see our families saved.

So, don't let Satan keep your children in the world by telling you lies that keep you in bondage to worry, doubt, and fear. Claim your family for the Lord and bring them out to worship the Lord in spirit and in truth.

Finally, Pharaoh declared his fourth form of worship. "Go, worship the LORD. Even your women and children may go with you; only leave your flocks and herds behind" (Exodus 10:24 NIV, *emphasis mine*).

Mackintosh's writings reveal that the first three forms of counterfeit worship showed Pharaoh's ploy to keep the Israelites connected to Egypt. First, to keep them in land, then to keep them near the land, and after that to keep their families. The last counterfeit worship, as Mackintosh explains, is Pharaoh's willingness to send the Israelites out of the land of Egypt but without any ability to worship (sacrifice to) God.[5]

For years Christian prosperity has been angrily opposed and called ungodly. Many in the Christian faith see money as evil when God says, "the love of money" is evil. Also, some believe that poverty somehow equates to humility. Based on Deuteronomy 28 and John 10:10, I equate poverty to the curse of the law, and Satan stealing.

Are you in debt to the world through loans and credit cards? My husband and I were until God showed us that He was unable to direct our money because we had bound it to the world's system. Through the law of sowing and reaping, God taught us how to get out of debt so that He could direct our money. In three and one-half years, we increased our giving of tithes and offerings and still paid off our debt of $150,000. Freedom from debt has enabled us to support more ministries and to leave our jobs to work full-time for God.

I am not condemning anyone for being in debt or for not having money. I want to encourage you. Let God's Word and His Spirit teach you how to become debt free.

God wants us to prosper but with right motives. He prospers us so that we can bless others, not so that we can have more "stuff." Prosperity is part of the covenant He has for those that seek Him (true worship).

God said it all about worship when His Spirit inspired these words:

I APPEAL to you therefore, brethren, *and* beg of
you in view of [all] the mercies of God, to make
a decisive dedication of your bodies [present-
ing all your members and faculties] as a living
sacrifice, holy (devoted, consecrated) and well
pleasing to God which is your reasonable (ra-
tional, intelligent) service *and* spiritual worship.
(Romans 12:1 Amp)

Through the Israelites, God shows us once again His
perfect deliverance. "He brought them forth also with
silver and gold: and *there was* not one feeble *person* among
their tribes" (Psalm 105:37). As a type and shadow, we
can see the total deliverance plan of God for His children.
Through Jesus Christ, we are saved. And as we surrender
our lives to Him by worshipping Him in spirit and in
truth, we will see the evidence of our born again spirit
manifested in every area of our lives. It truly is a triune
salvation: spirit, soul, and body as we die to self and live
in and through Christ.

Chapter Four

God Is Come to Prove You

And Moses said unto the people, Fear not: for
God is come to prove you,
and that his fear may be before your faces, that ye sin not.
Exodus 20:20

Categorizing Life's Events and Circumstances

I realize that I have hit a nerve in many Christians regarding their foundational beliefs of Who God is according to their understanding of the sovereignty of God, the authority of the believer, and how God accomplishes His plans and purposes here on earth. I believe much of the strife and confusion in the church concerning these beliefs is due to the lack of an intimate relationship with God. That explains why becoming a true worshipper is so important.

I have been cautioned *not* to categorize events and circumstances as "good" or "bad" based on my limited perspective. But I am not the one who did the categorizing. I am basing what I believe to be "good" or "bad" events or circumstances on the Word of God. God has told us in Deuteronomy 28 what are blessings and what are curses (See Appendix A: The Blessings

and Curses of the Law). Then He tells us in the New
Testament that we no longer have to live with the curses.

> Christ hath redeemed us from the curse of the
> law, being made a curse for us: for it is written,
> Cursed *is* every one that hangeth on a tree:
> That the blessing of Abraham might come
> on the Gentiles through Jesus Christ; that
> we might receive the promise of the Spirit
> through faith.
> (Galatians 3:13-14)

So when I read the lists of destructive events and
circumstances including sickness, disease, and poverty in
the curse of the law, I know that those things are "bad"
because God has said they are. In addition, I know I have
been set free from them because God has said so.

According to God, however, He has *not* done away
with the blessings of the law. So as we read the blessings,
we begin to see God's perfect will for us as we follow
after Him. In Christ we have become the heirs of all
His blessings. By grace through faith in our redeemer,
Jesus Christ, we have the blessings. And those blessings
become manifested in our lives as we renew our minds
and subject our bodies to God through the intimate
knowledge of Him. The Bible says,

> May blessing (praise, laudation, and eulogy) be
> to the God and Father of our Lord Jesus Christ

(the Messiah) Who has blessed us *in Christ* with
every spiritual (given by the Holy Spirit) blessing in the heavenly realm!
(Ephesians 1:3 Amp)

We no longer receive the blessings according to our
obedience to the rules and regulations of the law, but we
receive them by believing and acting on the Word of God.
And we can only do that by becoming true worshippers
(worshiping in spirit and truth).

Jesus said, "The thief cometh not, but for to
steal, and to kill, and to destroy: I am come that they
might have life, and that they might have *it* more
abundantly" (John 10:10). God said, "I call heaven
and earth to record this day against you, *that* I have
set before you life and death, blessings and cursing:
therefore choose life, that both thou and thy seed
may live" (Deuteronomy 30:19). According to these
Scriptures, God has given us the ability to determine
what is life and what is death; what is a blessing and
what is a curse; what is good and what is bad. And
then we are admonished to choose life.

Based on God's Word, we have assurance
that God means for us to have abundant life–His
blessings. And based on His Word, we know the thief
(Satan) means to steal those blessings even if he has
to kill and destroy us to do so. But did you notice
who is to know the difference and choose life? That's
right. We make the decision for life by believing and

receiving God's perfect will for us. This is why we are told to "Submit yourselves therefore to God. Resist the devil, and he will flee from you" (James 4:7). But if we believe that God uses evil events and circumstances to train His children, how do we know what is of God and what is of Satan? How do we know when to submit and when to resist? Without an intimate knowledge of God and an unwavering understanding of Who God is, this faith walk will become unbearably confusing. And we know that confusion does not come from God.

Scripture tells us the difference between the spiritually immature and the spiritually mature.

> For every one that useth milk *is* unskillful in the word of righteousness: for he is a babe.
> But strong meat belongeth to them that are of full age, *even* **those who by reason of use have their senses exercised to discern both good and evil.**
> (Hebrews 5:13-14, *emphasis mine*)

So we see it is necessary for us to grow in the Word and practice discerning what God has called good, and what He has called evil. God has said that if it is abundant life, it is good, but if it is stealing, killing, or destroying, it is evil. This knowledge enables us to become skilled at submitting to God and resisting the devil.

Temptation–Enticement to Sin

In the previous chapters, I have tried to show that tests (trials, proofs, temptations) will come, but those of God are not evil. They are for the purifying of our hearts by making decisions to obey Him with correct motives. We are being perfected in love by His "putting to proof" of our faith in Him. But if we are being tempted with evil (Satan applying pressure on us to abandon what we believe), God encourages us to ask Him for wisdom.

> If any of you lack wisdom, let him ask of God, that giveth to all *men* liberally, and upbraideth not; and it shall be given him.
> But let him ask in faith, nothing wavering. For he that wavereth is like a wave of the sea driven with the wind and tossed.
> For let not that man think that he shall receive any thing of the Lord.
> A double minded man *is* unstable in all his ways....
> Blessed *is* the man that endureth **temptation**: for when he is tried, he shall receive the crown of life, which the Lord hath promised to them that love him.
> Let no man say when he is **tempted**, I am **tempted** of God: for God cannot be **tempted** with evil, neither **tempteth** he any man:
> But every man is **tempted**, when he is drawn

away of his own lust, and enticed.

Then when lust hath conceived, it bringeth
forth sin: and sin, when it is finished, bringeth
forth death.

Do not err, my beloved brethern.

Every good gift and every perfect gift is from
above, and cometh down from the Father of
lights, with whom is no variableness, neither
shadow of turning.

(James 1:5-8 and 12-17, *emphasis mine*)

In the previous Scripture, *temptation* and *tempt* is
referring to "enticement to sin."[1] Also, the Scripture notes
that God cannot be enticed to sin, and He does not entice
us to sin. God is not the destroyer of our faith. Jesus is the
author and finisher of our faith. No, unbelief and doubt in
God's Word (questioning His character and nature) caused
by Satan's temptations is the destroyer of our faith.

Temptation–Test, Try, or Prove

Let us look at the word, *tempt*, in another Scripture.

AND IT came to pass after these things, that
God did **tempt** Abraham, and said unto him,
Abraham: and he said, Behold, *here I am*.
And he said, Take now thy son, thine only *son*
Isaac, whom thou lovest, and get thee into the
land of Moriah; and offer him there for a burnt

offering upon one of the mountains which I will
tell thee of.

(Genesis 22:1-2, *emphasis mine*)

Obviously, there must be another meaning for the
word *tempt* since God does not entice us to sin. In this
Scripture, *tempt* means to "test, try, or prove, put to the
proof."[2]

If we examine each of these words, we begin to
see clearly another application of the word *tempt*. The
following definitions were taking from the 1828 *American
Dictionary of the English Language* by Noah Webster.

> *Test*, v. t. To compare with a standard; to
> try; to prove the truth or genuineness of any
> thing by experiment or by some fixed principle
> or standard; as, to *test* the soundness of a prin-
> ciple; to test the validity of an argument.
>
> *Try*, v. t. To examine; to make experiment
> on; to prove by experiment. 2. To experience; to
> have knowledge by experience of. 7. To purify;
> to refine; as silver seven times tried.
>
> *Prove*, v. t. To try; to ascertain some un-
> known quality or truth by an experiment, or by
> a test or standard. Thus to prove the strength
> of gunpowder by experiment; we *prove* the
> strength or solidity of cannon by experiment.
> We *prove* the contents of a vessel by comparing
> it with a standard measure.[3]

Abraham, a Friend of God

By these definitions, we can see that God tempts or tests us for completely different reasons than Satan. As I said in previous chapters, God tests our obedience and our motives for purification of our hearts toward Him and His will. And if you are prepared for the tests, unbearable suffering does not have to be part of the process.

God's tests reveal nothing to God, for He knows all things. No, God's tests are for our benefit to reveal how much we have allowed His character and nature to manifest in our lives. God's tests reveal to us the standard by which we are living–either by the world's standard or by God's standard. God's tests show us how much we believe His Word and how much we are willing to live by it.

Notice that it says in Genesis 22:1, "And it came to pass after these things, that God did tempt Abraham...." After what things? Well, how about receiving the promised child, Isaac, after it seemed impossible by human standards.

By whose standard of measure had Abraham learned to trust? Was it by the world's standard, or was it by God's standard that showed the impossible as possible? God knew the answer to that question and through a test revealed this answer to Abraham. And Scripture reveals the answer to us.

> (As it is written, I have made thee a father of
> many nations,) before him whom he believed,

even God, who quickeneth the dead, and calleth
those things which be not as though they were.
Who against hope believed in hope, that he
might become the father of many nations,
according to that which was spoken, So shall
thy seed be.
And being not weak in faith, he considered not
his own body now dead, when he was about an
hundred years old, neither yet the deadness of
Sarah's womb:
He staggered not at the promise of God
through unbelief; but was strong in faith, giving glory to God;
And being fully persuaded that, what he had
promised, he was able also to perform.
And therefore it was imputed to him for
righteousness.
(Romans 4:17-22)

Through intimate relationship and fellowship,
Abraham had learned to trust God and live by His
standard. Abraham knew God, and Abraham was
a friend of God. James 2:23 clearly states, "… and
he was called the Friend of God." And how do
friendships develop? Friendships are established
through intimate relationship through sharing and
caring. True friends are willing to reveal who they
are with one another without fear. Their friendship is
apparent when God says to Abraham,

> Shall I hide from Abraham that thing which I do;
> Seeing that Abraham shall surely become a
> great and mighty nation, and all the nations of
> the earth shall be blessed in him?
> (Genesis 18:17-18)

God, in the image of a man, came to Abraham, and they ate and fellowshipped together. As Abraham drew near to God, their intimate relationship was revealed. As friends, God discussed specific plans with Abraham. The first discussion dealt with the birth of Isaac, the promised child. Later, they discussed the outcome of Sodom and Gomorrah.

Notice they had a two-way conversation. All the while, God was "putting to proof" the obedience and motives of Abraham's heart. First, He encouraged Abraham to believe and to be obedient to God's Word concerning the promised child through which "all the nations of the earth shall be blessed." Then God motivated Abraham to petition Him for the salvation of the righteous in Sodom and Gomorrah.

But this is not the first or the last time we see their close friendship revealed. The various ways Abraham greeted the Lord showed intimacy. In Genesis 18:2-3 Abraham ran to God, bowed before Him, and addressed Him as "My Lord." Abraham was very clear about who was passing by his tent. Intimate knowledge and experience with God enabled Abraham to recognize who he was entertaining.

Look at how Abraham greeted God in Genesis 22:1. After God called Abraham by name, Abraham confidently answers, "… Behold, *here* I *am*." Now compare that with Adam's response when God called to him in Genesis 3:9. Because of lost relationship and fellowship due to sin, fear came upon Adam, and he hid from God.

God is calling us by name, but what is our response? Do we know God as a friend and call out confidently and joyfully? Or do we shrink back in fear not understanding how much God loves us?

Faith in the Promiser

Now, what does all this have to do with God's tempting of Abraham? According to the movies, after God asked Abraham to sacrifice Isaac, Abraham wailed and travailed in anguish, shook his fists to the heavens, fell to the ground, and screamed, "No, not my son." But read the true account in Genesis 22. What happened after God commanded Isaac to be sacrificed? Scripture tells us,

> By faith Abraham, when God tested him, offered Isaac as a sacrifice. He who had re-
> ceived the promises was about to sacrifice his one and only son,
> Even though God had said to him, "It is through Isaac that your offspring will be reckoned."
> Abraham reasoned that God could raise the

dead, and figuratively speaking, he did receive
Isaac back from death.
(Hebrews 11:17-19 NIV)

Once again, by whose standard did Abraham live?
The world would have us believe that Abraham fell to
pieces. But the truth is that Abraham was fully persuaded
of God's faithfulness. Abraham had experience with the
Promiser, and he knew that God could not lie about His
promises. Therefore, Abraham's faith in God's Word
concerning the promised offspring through Isaac was
so strong that he imagined Isaac already sacrificed and
raised from the dead. Even before the event took place,
Abraham had already given Isaac up to the Lord but with
full assurance that God would give him back.

Still not convinced? Well, read this.

On the third day Abraham looked up and saw
the place in the distance.
He said to his servants, "Stay here with the don-
key while I and the boy go over there. We will
worship and then we will come back to you."
(Genesis 22:4-5 NIV)

As Abraham spoke these words, "we will worship
and then we will come back to you," his words
demonstrate why he has been hailed as the "Father of
Faith." He believed God's promise even in the face of
God's command to sacrifice the child of promise.

God tests our belief in Him by asking us to believe for the "impossible" by the world's standard. But Jesus assures us, "What is impossible with men is possible with God" (See Luke 18:27).

Abraham knew this without doubt because of his intimate relationship and previous experiences with God. Because of their friendship, God shared many desires of His heart with Abraham. Based on the following Scriptures, I believe that God even revealed His redemption plan for man to Abraham and Isaac. And once they believed on this future hope by faith, their salvation was secured.

Isaac asked Abraham where the lamb was for the burnt offering. Abraham, a prophet according to Genesis 20:7, answered, "God himself will provide the lamb for the burnt offering, my son..." (Genesis 22:8 NIV). Now compare that with what Jesus said. "... Your father Abraham rejoiced at the thought of seeing my day; **he saw it** and was glad" (John 8:56 NIV, *emphasis mine*).

We are told that Abraham believed God, and God credited it to him as righteousness. Because of this right standing with God, Abraham was living in the grace of God. In God's infinite grace and mercy, I believe God gave Abraham the ability to see the death and resurrection of "a son." Think about it. Had Abraham ever seen anyone raised from the dead? But Abraham had been living for years by God's standard that all things are possible with God. Hebrews 11:19 (NIV) tells us "Abraham reasoned that God could raise the dead, and figuratively speaking, he did receive Isaac back from death." Abraham weighed God's faithfulness in the past, with the promises God made about Isaac for the future, and without hesitation traveled to Mt. Moriah (future location of Jerusalem).

What I believe God showed Abraham, in his spirit, was the plan of redemption for the world through the sacrificial sin offering of God's son, Jesus Christ. I believe Abraham reasoned in his mind, however, that God had shown him the death and resurrection of his only son, Isaac. Abraham said these prophetic words to answer Isaac's question concerning the burnt offering, "God himself will provide a lamb for the burnt offering." God was speaking prophetically through Abraham about the substitutionary sacrifice that would be sent in the form of a ram caught in a bush and in the future as the sin offering of Jesus Christ nailed to the cross. But Abraham's reasoning told him, God provided Isaac supernaturally, and He will give Isaac back supernaturally.

Nevertheless, the most important fact is that Abraham remained faithful to the Promiser. In the end, Abraham is said to have seen Jesus' day. When did he see God's redemption plan? I believe when God provided the substitutionary ram, God flooded Isaac and Abraham's heart with the knowledge of our Savior, Jesus Christ. I believe God supernaturally showed them what was going to happen on that mount, which inspired Abraham to call that place Jehovah Jireh (The Lord will Provide).

Type and Shadow of God's Redemption Plan

This revelation was not just for Abraham and
Isaac. This is a type and shadow for us. We are told that
Abraham "offered up" Isaac as a sacrifice. But where
and when did Abraham make the offering? He made
the offering in his heart and mind as soon as he received
God's command. Then, after a three-day journey, the
son was received back from the dead at Mount Moriah.
This wonderful story gives us a window into the heart of
God. This story proves that God had purposed long ago
to sacrifice His only begotten Son for us so that we would
receive back the Son's life.

> I am crucified with Christ: nevertheless I live;
> yet not I, but Christ liveth in me: and the life
> which I now live in the flesh I live by faith of
> the Son of God, who loved me, and gave him-
> self for me.
> (Galatians 2:20)

Now, let us look at Isaac's role. Biblical
commentators suggest that Isaac was about 25 to 33
years old, and Abraham was about 125 to 133 years old.
This means Isaac willingly was bound and placed on
the altar, just as Jesus willingly laid down His life. Both
the father and the son gave up the son's life. And both,
Abraham and Isaac, received back the life of the son
in their hearts and minds when the angel of the Lord

showed them the ram that God provided as the true sacrifice. So, we clearly can see Isaac as a living sacrifice just as Jesus later became.

Because Abraham and Isaac display their willingness to die to self, they saw Jesus Christ's day as spoken of in John 8:56. They saw clearly the redemption plan of God for themselves and the world. If either one had refused to cooperate with God's will, God could not have completed His covenant with Abraham and work His redemption plan through the seed of Abraham. You see, God requires willing vessels to choose His way and His plan. So, we can see Abraham and Isaac as the living sacrifices that we are to be.

> THEREFORE, I urge you, brothers, in view of God's mercy, to offer your bodies as living sacrifices, holy and pleasing to God–this is your spiritual act of worship.
> Do not conform any longer to the pattern of this world, but be transformed by the renewing of your mind. Then you will be able to test and approve what God's will is–his good, pleasing and perfect will.
> (Romans 12:1-2 NIV)

Notice at the end of this test of obedience, God blessed and fulfilled the covenant with Abraham. Abraham's faith in God, obedience to God's will, and willingness to die to self–not withholding any earthly possession from God–made all that possible. Was the test a source of unbearable suffering on Abraham's part? No! He was already fully persuaded that God is able to do the impossible. God "proved" this vessel, Abraham. And Abraham met God's standard by which he was measured; a standard deemed impossible by human standard. Abraham, however, was intimately acquainted with God's standard. He had already experienced and received the impossible by having faith in God. He had a working knowledge of God's character, nature, and ways. This test was not to prove anything to God. Nothing is unknown to God. It served as another opportunity to prove to Abraham and to us that faith and belief in the Promiser makes God's promises a reality in our lives.

Lessons from the Israelites:
The Unseen Way Out

C. H. Mackintosh made this wonderful statement,
"...unbelief ever reasons. It leads us to interpret God in
the presence of the difficulty, instead of interpreting the
difficulty in the presence of God."[4]

Unlike Abraham, this statement characterizes the
Israelites and their inability to believe God. As the Lord
led the Israelites from Egypt in the form of a pillar of
cloud by day and a pillar of fire by night, He chose
not to lead them the shortest route but led them to the
wilderness. And to their frustration and eventual terror,
He even turned them toward the Red Sea seemingly
trapping them between the mountains and the sea. The
Israelites' apparent confusion enticed Pharaoh and the
Egyptians to pursue and try to enslave the Israelites once
again (See Exodus 13:17 and 14:9).

I have often heard that the Israelites' journey to the
Red Sea and into the wilderness is an example of how
God leads believers today into hard places to teach us
hard lessons. I do not believe that this is the case. Once
again, God does not tempt us with evil. This is not His
character or nature. What many fail to understand and
what the Bible clearly tells us in 1 Corinthians 10:11 is
that the lessons of the Israelites are to teach us so that
we do not make the same mistakes they did. So from

that perspective, let us now study the Israelites'
Red Sea experience.

First, God led the Israelites the longer route to
the Red Sea because of His compassionate, loving
nature. We are told that if He had led them into the
land of the Philistines, they would have feared war
and run back to Egypt.

> When Pharaoh let the people go, God led them
> not by way of the land of Philistines, although
> that was nearer; for God said, Lest the people
> change their purpose when they see war, and
> they return to Egypt.
> But God led the people around by way of the
> wilderness toward the Red Sea. And the Isra-
> elites went up marshaled [in ranks] out of the
> land of Egypt.
> (Exodus 13:17-18 Amp)

God knew they still had the minds of slaves and
did not have the ability to fight the necessary battles
to maintain their freedom. So, He protected them from
themselves through His wisdom and His ways.

We can see the application in our own lives. Once
we are saved, we must exchange our "old ideas of who
we are" with our "new identity in Jesus Christ." The
renewing of our minds with the Word of God can only
do this. We have to study to find out who we are in Him
(See Appendix B: In Christ Jesus). This enables us to

separate ourselves from the world and learn to become the army of Christ.

Also, we see that God began to lead the Israelites one way and then turned them another seemingly perilous way. God understood the heart of Pharaoh (Satan) and the Egyptians (the world). He knew that their hearts were forever hardened to God and His people. He further knew that any sign of weakness, such as appearing confused and trapped at the edge of the sea, would cause Pharaoh and his army to attack and try to enslave God's people once again (See Exodus 14:1-9). God would use the ever-hardening heart of Pharaoh to soundly defeat the Egyptians and show His glory to all the nations. He did this by the spectacular parting of the Red Sea. All the nations in the promised land would tremble and fear the God of Israel. They would not dare resist the Israelites as they claimed God's promised land (See Joshua 2:9-11).

Do you see how God's plans are perfect? "Trust in the LORD with all thine heart; and lean not unto thine own understanding. In all thy ways acknowledge him, and he shall direct thy paths. Be not wise in thine own eyes: fear the LORD, and depart from evil" (Proverbs 3:5-6).

One of the most insightful passages in the entire account of the Israelites' encounter at the Red Sea is "As Pharaoh approached, the Israelites looked up, and there were the Egyptians, marching after them. They were terrified and cried out to the LORD" (Exodus 14:10 NIV). This passage shows the unbelieving hearts of the Israelites.

God's people had just witnessed ten signs and wonders that brought about their deliverance from Egypt. And Psalm 105:37 tells us that they came out of Egypt wealthy and healthy. (Notice God did not prove them with poverty or sickness.) And wasn't the Lord, Jesus, personally guiding them? So, what was the reason for their doubting hearts? Why were they looking behind them when their miracle-working God was before them? Why were they looking behind them, when the unseen way out was before them? Why would they turn away from the perfect to gaze upon the imperfect?

Mackintosh's statement that was mentioned earlier answers these questions. "… unbelief ever reasons. It leads us to interpret God in the presence of the difficulty, instead of interpreting the difficulty in the presence of God."[5]

God had personally come down to walk with them every step of the way. Yet in His presence, they chose to look at their circumstance and cry out faithless words of destruction. But God in His faithfulness spoke through Moses,

> …Fear ye not, stand still, and see the salvation of the LORD, which he will show to you today: for the Egyptians whom ye have seen today, ye shall see them again no more for ever.
> The LORD shall fight for you, and ye shall hold your peace.…
> And the angel of God, which went before the

camp of Israel, removed and went behind them;
and the pillar of the cloud went from before
their face, and stood behind them:
And it came between the camp of the Egyptians
and the camp of Israel; and it was a cloud and
darkness *to them*, but it gave light by night *to*
these: so that the one came not near the other
all the night.
(Exodus 14:13-14 and 19-20)

Mackintosh points out two significant positions in the passages of Scripture. Standing still is the command given to believers in tough situations. Instead of trying to do for ourselves, we must cease from our own efforts and enter the rest of God. Only when we give up our self-effort can God go to work on our behalf. Only after we demonstrate our faith through belief in Him, can He move on our behalf.

That brings us to the second position. When we take our hands off the problem, God will then separate us from it by placing Himself in the position of a sword and shield. God physically positioned Himself between the Israelites and their enemies in Exodus. But as New Testament believers, our battles are spiritual. We battle using the Word as our sword and faith in the Word as our shield (See Ephesians 6:10-17).

One of the most remarkable aspects of the Lord's move is the effect God has on the human heart. When the Lord moved between His people and the Egyptians, the Israelites saw "light" while the Egyptians saw only "darkness." An analogy that best describes this effect is "the same sun that softens wax can also harden clay." So depending on the condition of our hearts, we either allow the truth of God's Word to humble us or make us proud and rebellious. From Exodus 14:20 we can see that God and His Word had made the Egyptians extremely proud thereby causing their hearts to become hard and unchangeable.

Now, at this point, some may still believe that God leads His children into hard places to teach them a lesson. And that somehow He needs Satan's help to teach us. I can agree, however, only in part. I do believe that God leads us. I do believe that there will be hard places. But, I believe that God will prepare us for the trip, and He certainly does not need assistance in training His children (especially with someone or something evil). Let us look again at the Israelites for an example.

God had a perfect purpose for leading the Israelites the way He did. All that God required of the Israelites was to trust and obey. And God had given them many reasons to be able to trust Him. But did God entice Pharaoh to attack the Israelites for the express purpose of testing or tempting His children? My answer, based on Scripture, is a resounding no!

When we read Romans 8 and 9, we can see that Paul goes to great length to explain the sovereignty of God in relationship to predestination based on God's foreknowledge of people.

> For those God foreknew he also predestined to
> be conformed to the likeness of his Son, that he
> might be the firstborn among many brothers.
> And those he predestined, he also called; those
> he called, he also justified; those he justified, he
> also glorified.
> What, then, shall we say in response to this? If
> God is for us, who can be against us?
> (Romans 8:29-31 NIV)

Then in Romans 9 we are given great insight as
to what is meant by predestination based on God's
foreknowledge. Paul explains (verse 14 and 15) that God
is not unjust. God told Moses He would have mercy and
compassion on whom He pleases. Paul said (verse 22)
that if God chose to have mercy on the sinful (which He
did through Jesus Christ), that no one is to question His
fairness or His justice.

> For Scripture says to Pharaoh: "I raised you
> up for this very purpose, that I might display
> my power in you and that my name might be
> proclaimed in all the earth."
> Therefore God has mercy on whom he wants to have
> mercy, and he hardens whom he wants to harden.
> (Romans 9:17-18 NIV)

God is the only One Who knows the heart of a man
(See 1 Samuel 16:7). He is the only One Who knows the

"Elect according to the foreknowledge…" (1 Peter 1:2). And He clearly tells us what He does with that knowledge. "…God resisteth the proud and giveth grace unto the humble" (James 4:6). This makes more clear His statement to Moses: "Therefore God has mercy on whom he wants to have mercy, and he hardens whom he wants to harden" (Romans 9:18 NIV).

These three scriptures explain that God does not extend mercy or justice arbitrarily but that He deals with people according to the condition of their hearts.

> …so they are without excuse:
> Because that, when they knew God, they glori-fied *him* not as God, neither were thankful; but became vain in their imaginations, and their foolish heart was darkened.…
> And even as they did not like to retain God in *their* knowledge, God gave them over to a reprobate mind, to do those things which are not convenient;
> (Romans 1:20b-21 and 28)

As we apply this to Pharaoh, we can see that on nine separate occasions Pharaoh hardened his heart toward God. Knowing through foreknowledge that Pharaoh would not change his mind, God just gave him over to his "reprobate mind." God allowed Satan's instrument of evil to have his own way. As a result, God resisted the Egyptians, and He delivered His children with such a spectacular show of power that all the nations trembled (See Joshua 2:9-10).

All His children had to do is this:

> ...Fear ye not, stand still, and see the salvation
> of the Lord, which he will show to you today:
> for the Egyptians whom ye have seen today, ye
> shall see them again no more for ever.
> The Lord shall fight for you, and ye shall hold
> your peace.
> (Exodus 14:13-14)

If we, as God's children, truly had a revelation of God's love toward us, we would not fear no matter the circumstance. The knowledge of God's perfect love would disable the power of fear. Thereby, allowing us to stand still in His perfect peace, believing that God will most surely deliver us from every evil by humbling our hearts with the steadfast commitment to obey Him.

Abraham was fully persuaded that God is faithful to His Word, and righteousness was credited to him. The Israelites continually doubted God; however, and it caused them to die in the wilderness. We are assured the victory in Jesus Christ. The Word says,

> These things I have spoken unto you, that in me
> ye might have peace. In the world ye shall have
> tribulation: but be of good cheer; I have over-
> come the world.

> There hath no temptation taken you but such as
> is common to man: but God *is* faithful, who will
> not suffer you to be tempted above that ye are
> able; but will with the temptation also make a
> way to escape, that ye may be able to bear *it*.
> (John 16:33 and 1 Corinthian 10:13)

In Him, we have victory over all the works of the devil. In Him, every situation has a way of escape. Just like the Israelites, we have to decide whether to stay focused on the Red Sea (God's unseen way out until it becomes visible by trusting and relying on God's grace and mercy) or whether to turn our attention to the approaching Egyptians (the seemingly life-threatening circumstances of this world–both spiritual and physical).

Notice that the Israelites did not see the way out until they took that first step of faith. Once they became fully persuaded, God could make a way for them. God's way is the only way. The cross always requires us to move toward His path of salvation and redemption. Now, when I find myself in a hard place, God gently speaks these words to me. "Which way are you looking?"

Chapter Five

God Is Glorified in Him

Therefore, when he was gone out, Jesus said,
*Now is the Son of man glorified, and **God is glorified in him.***
John 13:31

Fully Persuaded and Prepared

When reading the account of Jesus in the Garden of Gethsemane the night before His sacrifice, and the account of Abraham in preparing to sacrifice Isaac, we see very different reactions. Did both know their obedience to God was being tested? Yes. Had both been living by God's standard and fully persuaded that God was able to do the impossible? Yes. We can see through Scripture that both were prepared for God's test of obedience. So, what was it about Jesus' test of obedience unto death that brought such agonizing sorrow? The major difference I see between the two tests was that Jesus knew His test required the spiritual separation from His Father.

Romans 6:23 tells us, "For the wages of sin *is* death but the gift of God is eternal life through Jesus Christ our Lord." John 17:3 defines eternal life as knowing God intimately. So death, as payment for sin, would be the opposite. Jesus understood the wages of sin He would have to pay (a death that involved broken relationship and fellowship with the Father) in order to become the final sin offering as well as scapegoat for all of our sins.

We, as Christians, must come to understand and believe that as a God-man, Jesus experienced all the thoughts, emotions, self-will, and pain of a man. Seeing Him this way will enable us to see how Jesus' battle in the Garden of Gethsemane was a battle of bringing the flesh into submission to the Father's will. Remember, as God, He could have commanded legions of angels to fight for Him. Instead, He restrained His flesh (dying to self), and fulfilled the will of the Father unto death in all three areas: spirit, soul, and body.

We are assured by Jesus' own words that He understood and trusted in His Father's love. Jesus was committed to God's plan to save mankind.

> Therefore doth my Father love me, because I
> lay down my life, that I might take it again.
> No man taketh it from me, but I lay it down of
> myself. I have power to lay it down, and I have
> power to take it again. This commandment
> have I received of my Father.
> (John 10:17-18)

Yet, Jesus also understood that God's plan required Him to leave the comfort of God's relationship and fellowship to surrender Himself to the powers of this world. Jesus tells the religious leaders, "When I was daily with you in the temple, ye stretched forth no hands against me: but this is your hour, and the power of darkness" (Luke 22:53).

That night in the Garden of Gethsemane, He saw the cup of wrath that He must drink without the comfort of His Father's love. The knowledge of this made Jesus sorrowful unto death. That explains why He cried out, "…Father, if thou be willing, remove this cup from me: nevertheless not my will, but thine, be done" (Luke 22:42).

What does this reveal to us? It shows us that Jesus was a man. People want to dismiss many of the works of Jesus on earth by saying, "Well, easy enough for Jesus to do; He is God." But they fail to see that He was all God and all man. He experienced life on this earth as a man. He cried; he laughed; he was tempted to sin in every way we are. And in those times of temptation, He went to His Father for encouragement and strength.

Did God answer Jesus in the garden that night? Yes! Just as in the wilderness after fasting forty days and being tempted by Satan, God sent an angel to strengthen Him. Praise God that Jesus, our advocate, understands us. He knows how we suffer temptation but assures us that the Father has supplied us with what we need to gain victory.

A Love So Great

"Greater love hath no man than this, that a man lay down his life for his friends" (John 15:13). Jesus showed the deep abiding love for His Father and for mankind by voluntarily laying down His life for us in obedience to His Father's will. In this selfless act of unconditional love, Jesus demonstrated how to love God and others. Jesus' example shows us love is not a feeling or an emotion but an action that brings death to our self-will and life through obedience to God's perfect will.

God is love, and Jesus is the perfect representation of God's love towards us. Jesus always showed us the Father (See John 4:32, 33, 34; 5:19, 30; 6:38; 7:16, 28, 29; 8:16, 26, 28, 29; 10:17, 18, 30, 38; 12:49; and 14:8, 9, 24).

As God's unconditional love towards us becomes more of a reality in our lives, our focus on "self" will become less important. Becoming fully persuaded that God is for us and not against us will give us confidence in Him alone. Dying to self-will becomes easier as the life of Christ grows greater within us through the power of the Holy Spirit. As the Holy Spirit teaches us of God's love for us, we will see our willingness to listen and to obey His Word increase proportionately.

Someone once told me that "one is never in control or out of control; one is always under control." We are either under the control of God or of Satan. We ultimately make a choice who controls our lives. God has told us to choose life. So, anytime we choose death, Satan is able to steal, kill, and destroy.

Some in challenging circumstances may say, "Right now, I am being controlled by a sickness or a disastrous circumstance. I didn't choose to have sickness or disaster wreck my life; it just happened."

Keep in mind that just living in a fallen world can bring some awful things into our lives. How do we respond? Do we resist it by speaking the Word of God concerning the situation as God has instructed us? Or do we look at the circumstance and speak what we see? We make the choice between speaking life or speaking death!

If we truly have a revelation of God's love, we will speak what God says. But if we do not know the love of God, we will speak what "self" has to say. "Self" will speak faithless words of defeat especially if an illness or circumstance lingers. Then, "self" will give up and make God responsible for our failure. "Self" will say God didn't heal or deliver because He is using the situation for a training seminar. Consequently, Satan is allowed by those faithless words to twist and to make what is evil seem good and loving.

At this point, some may say, "But I learned so much from that tragedy. It must have been God Who caused that to happen, so I could experience a closer walk with Him." While it may be true that God caused all things to work together for good (See Romans 8:28), He was not the One Who caused the tragedy. He is a faithful God Who will never leave us or forsake us. But again, anything that attempts to "steal, kill, or destroy" is not God.

Once, in response to this same argument that God brings bad things into our lives to teach us, I reminded a person that if an earthly father did what she said God was doing, the father would be put in prison for child abuse. Then I said, "If God really is doing these horrible things to teach us, why are we trying so hard to get out of them? Let's just stay in those situations to really learn God's lessons." I finished with, "Why would anyone serve a God like she was describing?"

She countered by asking me how I would explain people being martyred while doing the will of God. I replied, "Apples and oranges!" The Bible definitely says all Christians will experience suffering, but the suffering is not the sicknesses, diseases, and the many other tragedies under the curse of the law.

Look again at those sufferings of evil we have been redeemed from due to the finished work of Jesus: "sin, sickness/disease, poverty, bad habits, lack of spiritual power, and failure in prayer."[1]

Now, compare those to the suffering that all Christians are told they will go through for the Gospel's sake:

> Persecution; reviling (contemptuous languages) and slander; false accusations; scourgings (whipping, punishing, afflicting); rejection by men; hatred by the world; hatred by relatives; martyrdoms; temptations; shame; imprisonments; tribulations; stonings; beatings; a spectacle to men; misunderstanding; necessities, defamation, and despisings; trouble, affliction, distresses, tumults, labors, watchings, fastings, and evil reports; reproaches; trials; and satanic oppositions.[2]

What are Christians to Suffer?

Jesus said,

> If you were of the world, the world would love
> his own: but because ye are not of the world,
> but I have chosen you out of the world, there-
> fore the world hateth you.
> Remember the word that I said unto you. The
> servant is not greater than his lord. If they
> have persecuted me, they will also persecute
> you; if they have kept my saying, they will
> keep yours also.
> But all these things will they do unto you for
> my name's sake, because they know not him
> that sent me.
> (John 15:19-21)

The Word tells us that when we testify about Jesus Christ to a lost and dying world, we are to be prepared for a certain amount of persecution. If we are not experiencing persecution, Scripture tells us that we are not fully committing our lives to Christ. Making Jesus not only our Savior but also our Lord will cause us to follow the leading of the Holy Spirit. As a result, we will encounter resistance from the world. Read the accounts of the apostles in Acts.

So what brings this persecution Jesus promised would come? Persecutions come as a result of living our

lives as Christ's witnesses. Surprisingly, the words *witness*
and *martyr* were translated from the same Greek word,
martus. In the legal sense, a *martus* is one who can give an
eye witness account (i.e. any of the disciples that knew Jesus
personally). In the historical sense, a *martus* is one who
serves by testimony–faithfully interpreting God's Word.
Finally, in the ethical sense, a *martus* is one who, after His
example, has proved the strength and genuineness of his
faith in Christ by undergoing a violent death.[3]

The definition of *martus* helps us to see that the
words *witness* and *martyr* have a much broader meaning
than many have realized. As witnesses for Jesus Christ,
we are to be daily martyred albeit to a lesser degree than
those who sacrifice their physical lives. It mean that each
time we choose God's ways and not our own, we must die
to self. We must stop fearing the opinions of men and their
persecution and live our lives circumspectly before God.
By the power of the Holy Spirit and our decision to serve
God, our lives become a living testament to men about the
goodness and love of God. We give up our self-life (trying
to live for God) for the Christ-centered life (allowing God
to live His life through us). Then God's abundant grace is
available to us in order to do all that He has planned and
purposed for us.

So, by looking at martyrdom as a witness for Christ that
requires dying to self, it helps us to understand Paul's testimony.

> I am crucified with Christ: nevertheless I live; yet
> not I, but Christ liveth in me: and the life which I

now live in the flesh I live by the faith of the Son
of God, who loved me, and gave himself for me.
(Galatians 2:20)

Paul understood the requirement necessary
to live like Christ. The requirement is to live the
exchanged life of Christ and not just to live a better
version of our old life in our own effort. Truly, we are
a new creation through Christ.

Once, after reading the Scriptures in Exodus 33 and
34 in which Moses asked to see God's glory, I was so
overwhelmed that I said with great conviction, "Show me
your glory, God." Immediately, the Holy Spirit answered,
"Look in the mirror."

I was amazed when I realized that we are literally
God's glory here on earth. How much God is able to
work the life of Christ into our lives is proportionate
to how much of God's glory the world will see. We are
living testaments and ambassadors for Christ. We need to
think that way and act accordingly.

The Question of Martyrs

Okay, back to the question asked earlier. Why
does God allow His saints to be martyred to the point
of physical death? First, let us look at the first martyr
mentioned under the new dispensation of grace. Through
the martyr, Stephen, we see that persecution most
certainly abounded as a result of his testimony about

Christ. Also, we are told what Stephen saw as he laid down his life for Christ Jesus.

> But he, being full of the Holy Ghost, looked up
> stedfastly into heaven, and saw the glory of God,
> and Jesus standing on the right hand of God,
> And said, Behold, I see the heavens opened, and
> the Son of man standing on the right hand of God.
> Then they cried out with a loud voice, and stopped
> their ears, and ran upon him with one accord,
> And cast *him* out of the city, and stoned *him*:
> and the witnesses laid down their clothes at a
> young man's feet, whose name was Saul.
> And they stoned Stephen, calling upon God,
> and saying, Lord Jesus, receive my spirit.
> And he kneeled down, and cried with a loud
> voice, Lord, lay not this sin to their charge. And
> when he had said this, he fell asleep.
> (Acts 7:55-60)

This should be of great encouragement to us. God will never leave us or forsake us. Through God's merciful grace, Stephen had a vision of his future reward that caused his soul to be filled with peace. So much so that he was able to ask the Lord to forgive his enemies.

God answered that prayer through the conversion of Saul. Saul (Paul) was there as Stephen was martyred, but, later, he became one of the most "on fire" converts that ever lived. He not only brought the "good news" of salvation to the Gentiles, but also wrote much of the New Testament proclaiming the "good news" to future generations.

I would say that Stephen's "steadfastness to the truth" and "open display of love toward his enemies" was a powerful witness to God's grace. And only by God's grace shed abroad in our hearts through Christ Jesus can we accomplish such extraordinary works. We have to stop seeing ourselves as mere men (See 1 Corinthians 3:1-3). As Stephen, we are to be full of the Holy Spirit Who enables us to do the works of the Father. If we continue to see ourselves as mere men, we will fall into wrong thoughts about who we are. In Christ we will have God's grace when we need it–not a second before. That explains why we are told not to be concerned about tomorrow, for tomorrow has enough worries of its own. The grace we need is always present for the day, the hour, the minute, the second we need it.

By understanding truths about God's faithfulness, His abundance of grace through the finished work of Jesus, and the power of the Holy Spirit, we will face any tasks great or small with the vision Stephen was given. So what if it doesn't always feel good? Look Who is backing us–the entire Godhead. So what if it doesn't look safe? God's grace is sufficient. Paul wrote,

> For our light affliction, which is but for a mo-
> ment, worketh for us a far more exceeding *and*
> eternal weight of glory;

While we look not at the things which are seen,
but at the things which are not seen: for the
things which are seen *are* temporal; but the
things which are not seen *are* eternal.
(2 Corinthians 4:17-18)

Let us look at Paul's light afflictions.

...I have worked much harder, been in prison
more frequently, been flogged more severely,
and been exposed to death again and again.
Five times I received from the Jews the forty
lashes minus one.
Three times I was beaten with rods, once I was
stoned, three times I was shipwrecked, I spent a
night and a day in the open sea,
I have been constantly on the move. I have been
in danger from rivers, in danger from bandits,
in danger from my own countrymen, in danger
from Gentiles; in danger in the city, in danger
in the country, in danger at sea; and in danger
from false brothers.
I have labored and toiled and have often gone
without sleep; I have known hunger and thirst
and have often gone without food; I have been
cold and naked.
Besides everything else, I face daily the pressure of my concern for all the churches.
(2 Corinthians 11:23-28 NIV)

Paul called these sufferings *"light afflictions."* But we know there were times Paul grew weary because he later tells us he pleaded with God three times to remove *"a thorn in his flesh."* If we do our homework, we find that the Bible only refers to *"a thorn in the flesh"* as people who bring persecution against God's people. (See Numbers 33:55, Joshua 23:13, and Judges 2:3)

Paul used the figurative language, *a thorn in the flesh,* to describe the people Satan stirred up against him to keep him from spreading the Gospel to all the nations. This expression was used much like we use the expression, *"he or she is a pain in the neck."* Does our modern day expression mean we have a pain in our neck? No! This idiom or figure of speech has the same meaning as Paul's to express a negative feeling about someone or something.

Paul writes,

> And lest I should be exalted above measure through the abundance of the revelations, there was given to me **a thorn in the flesh, the messenger of Satan** to buffet me, lest I should be exalted above measure.
> For this thing I besought the Lord thrice, that it might depart from me.
> And he said unto me, **My grace is sufficient for thee: for my strength is made perfect in weakness**. Most gladly therefore will I rather glory in my infirmities, that the power of Christ may rest upon me.

> Therefore I take pleasure in infirmities, in
> reproaches, in necessities, in persecutions, in
> distresses for Christ's sake: for when I am weak,
> then am I strong.
> (2 Corinthians 12:7-10, *emphasis mine*)

Traditional teaching purports that the thorn in Paul's flesh was something that God brought upon Paul (whether it be sickness, disease, or persecution) to keep Paul humble. From a practical point of view, why would God make it difficult for Paul to preach the revelation that Jesus Christ restored both Jews' and Gentiles' relationship and fellowship with our heavenly Father by winning the victory over Satan? Even more impractical is the notion that God used a defeated enemy, the messenger (angel) of Satan, to buffet Paul from spreading this "good news."

Look again at the list of sufferings Paul experienced. I am sure in times of exhaustion and pain that Paul cried out to God for a release from these persecutions and dangers. We have many examples of God's men and women doing the same (i.e. Elijah running from Jezebel). But through the power of God's Word and Spirit, we see the strength of God's people restored.

God is telling Paul and us that His grace (power) will enable His witnesses (martyrs) to endure any task that God has for them. The moment God's people choose to acknowledge that they can do all things through Christ (the Anointed One and

His Anointing) and that nothing is impossible with God, they cease being "mere men."

God could have asked Paul these questions, "Which way are you looking? Are you looking at your circumstances in the light of your own self-sufficiency or in the light of your abundant God?" And Paul tells us what his answer to those questions would be. "...When I am weak, then am I strong." God is glorified in us through the life of Christ that lives in us.

Reading other writings of Paul, confirms that every believer is to be glorified through the life they live in Christ.

> [For my determined purpose is] that I may know Him [that I may progressively become more deeply and intimately acquainted with Him, perceiving and recognizing and understanding the wonders of His Person more strongly and more clearly], and that I may in that same way come to know the power outflowing from His resurrection [which it exerts over believers], and that I may so share his sufferings as to be continually transformed [in spirit into His likeness even] to His death, [in the hope] That if possible I may attain to the [spiritual and moral] resurrection [that lifts me] out from among the dead [even while in the body]. Not that I have now attained [this ideal], or have already been made perfect, but I press on to lay hold of (grasp) *and* make my own, that

for which Christ Jesus (the Messiah) has laid
hold of me *and* made me His own.

I do not consider, brethren, that I have captured
and made it my own [yet]; but one thing I do [it
is my one aspiration]: forgetting what lies behind and straining forward to what lies ahead,
I press on toward the goal to win the [supreme
and heavenly] prize to which God in Christ
Jesus is calling us upward.

So let those [of us] who are spiritually mature
and full-grown have this mind *and* hold these
convictions; and if in any respect you have a
different attitude of mind, God will make that
clear to you also.

(Philippians 3:10-15 Amp)

Jesus, Sorrowful unto Death

With all this said, we can see that Christ's
exchanged life in us, the fullness of Holy Spirit in us
and upon us (the anointing), and God's abundant grace
enable us to be witnesses (martyrs) for the Gospel's
sake. So, even unto death, God will faithfully sustain us.
Historical accounts report that those in the early church
sang as they were being crucified.

What accounts for their joy? Could it be that they
saw what Stephen saw by God's grace and mercy? Their
reward was opened before them: the glory of God and
the blessing of heaven seen. Paul said,

For me to live is Christ [His life in me], and to
die is gain [the gain of the glory of eternity].
But I am hard pressed between the two. My
yearning desire is to depart (to be free of this
world, to set forth) and be with Christ, for that
is far, far better.
(Philippians 1:21 and 23 Amp)

"This is my commandment, That ye love one
another, as I have loved you. Greater love hath no man
than this, that a man lay down his life for his friends"
(John 15:12-13). These words of Jesus' have brought joy
to countless that have followed this commandment. This
brings us back to the initial question at the beginning of
this chapter. So, what was it about Jesus' test of obedience
unto death that brought such agonizing sorrow?

Matthew Henry answered this question. Henry
observed that attached to Jesus' cross was the curse of the
law. But attached to the martyred saints' crosses are the
blessings of God.[4]

The sinless Jesus experienced the separation from
the Father for our sins, so we could receive the Father's
blessings. The curse of the law was crucified (put to
death) so that we could become sons and daughters to
our heavenly Father and receive all the benefits of our
inheritance of glory.

If we meditate on what Jesus did and truly believe
He gave up everything for us, we will begin to glorify the
Father through praise and worship no matter what we

have to go through. Jesus took on the sins of the world, was crucified, was buried, and suffered separation from the Father so we could be freed from all the works of Satan. Even in the suffering Jesus said would come to all Christians, we are assured that His grace is sufficient to see us through it.

So, Jesus glorified the Father, and the Father was glorified in Jesus. And now, we are glorified in Jesus, and Jesus is glorified in us. Praise God! We are no longer "mere men."

Lessons from the Israelites:
The Cross at the Red Sea
Killed the Egyptians but Not the Amalekites

Before investigating the types and shadows
represented in the Israelites' crossing at the Red Sea
and their battle with the Amalekites, let us first look at
some of the Passover requirements that typifies God's
redemptive plan. C. H. Mackintosh beautifully expresses
the Passover's spiritual applications.

> Leaven is, invariably, used, throughout
> scripture, as emblematical of evil.... "The feast
> of unleavened bread" is the type of that practi-
> cal separation from evil which is the proper re-
> sult of being washed from our sins in the blood
> of the Lamb, and the proper accompaniment of
> communion with His sufferings.... The Israelite
> did not put away leaven in order to be saved,
> but because he was saved; and if he failed to
> put away leaven, it did not raise the question
> of security through the blood, but simply of fel-
> lowship with the assembly.
> ...Practical holiness, though not the basis
> of our salvation, is intimately connected with
> our enjoyment thereof.... The blood is on the

lintel, but the leaven within their borders keeps
them from enjoying the security which the
blood provides. The allowance of evil destroys
our fellowship, though it does not break the
link which binds our souls eternally to God....[5]

Also, Mackintosh helps us to understand why
the Israelites were commanded to eat the roasted lamb
with bitter herbs.

If the roasted lamb expressed Christ's
endurance of the wrath of God in His own
Person, on the cross, the bitter herbs express
the believer's recognition of the truth that He
"suffered for us." "The chastisement of our
peace was upon him, and with his stripes we
are healed" (Isaiah 53:5).[6]

Mackintosh not only shows us the spiritual
significances of the Israelites eating the roasted lamb with
bitter herbs and unleavened bread in shelters protected
by the blood of the lamb, but he also draws our attention
to how they were to dress.

They were to eat it as a people prepared to leave behind them the land of death
and darkness, wrath and judgment, to move
onward toward the land of promise–their
destined inheritance.... The girded loins

bespoke intense separation from all around them, together with a readiness to serve. The shod feet declared their preparedness to leave that scene; while the staff was the expressive emblem of a pilgrim people, in the attitude of leaning on something outside themselves.... marked as a holy people, a crucified people, a watchful and diligent people.[7]

That Passover night God brought His children out of darkness into His glorious light by the blood of the Lamb. Along with their deliverance from slavery, their wealth and health were restored (See Psalm 105:37). God had prepared not only the children of Israel for the journey but also had given them the provisions to go.

But as with all who experience God's deliverance through the finished work of the Passover Lamb, we must allow God to lead us into the truth of who we are in Christ. We can see this truth through the Israelites' successful crossing of the Red Sea. God shows us in this spectacular scene at the Red Sea how we as born-again children of God must have a personal revelation of the cross, the burial, and the resurrection.

Mackintosh made the following observations about the cloud and the sea.

The cloud and the sea were to them what the cross and grave of Christ are to us. The cloud secured them from their enemies; the

sea separated them from Egypt: the cross, in
like manner, shields us from all that could be
against us, and we stand at heaven's side of the
empty tomb of Jesus.

The believer is not merely separated from
this present evil world, by the cross of Christ;
but he is quickened out of the grave of Christ,
"raised up together, and made to sit together
with Christ in heavenlies" (Ephesians 2:5-6).[8]

Mackintosh observed this about the Israelites'
triumphant arrival on the other side of the Red Sea.

It was not until, as a saved people, they
found themselves surrounded by the fruits of
God's salvation, that the triumphal hymn burst
forth from the whole redeemed assembly. It was
when they emerged from their significant baptism "in the cloud and the sea," and were able
to gaze upon the rich spoils of victory, which
lay scattered around them, that six hundred
thousand voices were heard chanting the song
of victory. The waters of the Red Sea rolled
between them and Egypt, and they stood on the
shore as a fully delivered people, and, therefore,
they were able to praise Jehovah.

In this, as in everything else, they were
our types. We, too, must know ourselves as
saved, in the power of death and resurrection,

before ever we can present clear and intelligent worship.... The Spirit of God reveals, with unmistakable clearness, in the Word, that the Church is united to Christ in death and resurrection; and, moreover, that a risen Christ, at God's right hand, is the measure and pledge of the Church's acceptance. When this is believed, it conducts the soul entirely beyond the region of doubt and uncertainty. How can the Christian doubt when he knows that he is continually represented before the throne of God by an Advocate, even "Jesus Christ the righteous?" It is the privilege of the very feeblest member of the Church of God to know that he was represented by Christ on the cross; that all his sins were confessed, borne, judged, and atoned for there. This is a divine reality, and, when laid hold of by faith, must give peace.... It is all about Jehovah.[9]

The Israelites were filled with true worship due to the victory only God could achieve for them. No one but God was responsible for removing what once threatened to kill them. Safe and secure on the other side, they could see Pharaoh and the Egyptians soundly defeated by their faithful God, Jehovah.

Certainly Jesus has done the same for us. Jesus "...having disarmed the powers and authorities, he made a public spectacle of them, triumphing over them by the cross" (Colossians 2:15 NIV). Jesus fully dealt with our sin and buried our past, present, and future sins deep in the watery grave much like the Egyptians. Now, we are raised from this baptism in Him with our minds set on the promised land.

One can see through the illustration of the Red Sea crossing how important water baptism is to a Christian's identity. By sharing in this public act of humility, we become fully persuaded of our membership into the body of Christ. We willingly partake in His crucifixion, death, and resurrection so that in our new identity, we can become effective witnesses. Our old man is left dead along the shore as we walk out onto the other side. As we journey to God's promised land, we are committed to completing God's purpose and plan for our lives. We are diligent to guard our hearts against pride as God uses us in powerful ways. We are quick to understand that *the body of Christ is not better because of our membership, but we are better because of our membership in the body of Christ.*

As the Israelites carry on with God, eventually we are given another glimpse of Christ crucified. Mackintosh eloquently describes the scene in Exodus 17.

> It was when the Rock of ages was cleft by the hand of Jehovah, that the flood-gates of eternal love were thrown wide open, and perishing sinners invited by the testimony of the

Holy Ghost to "drink abundantly," drink deeply, drink freely. "The gift of the Holy Ghost" is
the result of the Son's accomplished work upon
the cross. "The promise of the Father" could not
be fulfilled until Christ had taken His seat at the
right hand of the majesty in the heavens, having
wrought out perfect righteousness, answered
all the claims of holiness, magnified the law
and made it honourable, borne the unmitigated
wrath of God against sin, exhausted the power
of death and deprived the grave of its victory....
This is the true foundation of the church's
peace, blessedness, and glory, for ever.[10]

Mackintosh uses passages from the book of John that
parallel this scene in the desert. Jesus spoke these words.

But whosoever drinketh of the water that I shall
give him shall never thirst; but the water that
I shall give him shall be in him a well of water
springing up into everlasting life....
...If any man thirst, let him come unto me,
and drink.
He that believeth on me, as the scripture
hath said, out of his belly shall flow rivers of
living water.
(But this spake he of the Spirit, which they
that believe on him should receive: for the
Holy Ghost was not yet *given*; because that

> Jesus was not yet glorified.)
> (John 4:14 and 7:37-39)

We can see that the water pouring from the struck rock was representative of the Holy Spirit being poured out once Christ was gloried. Notice that once the Israelites drank this water, they were required to do something new. They were required to fight the Amalekites. "And Moses said unto Joshua, Choose us out men, and go out, fight with Amalek: tomorrow I will stand on the top of the hill with the rod of God in mine hand" (Exodus 17:9).

Until this point, God had fought all their battles, and His only command to the Israelites was to "stand still and see the salvation of the Lord." So, why were they now required to fight the Amalekites? Mackintosh answers this question by first explaining the difference between Pharaoh and Amalek.

> Pharaoh and Amalek represent two different powers or influences; Pharaoh represents the hindrance to Israel's deliverance from Egypt; Amalek represents the hindrance to their walk with God through the wilderness. Pharaoh used the things of Egypt to keep Israel from serving the Lord; he, therefore, prefigures Satan, who uses "this present evil world" against the people of God. Amalek, on the other hand, stands before us as the type of

the flesh. He was the grandson of Esau, who preferred a mess of pottage to the birthright (See Genesis 36:12). He [Amalek] was the first who opposed Israel, after their baptism "in the cloud and in the sea."[11]

What does the battle with the Amalekites have to do with drinking the spiritual water from the spiritual rock? Mackintosh explains.

The connection between his [Amalek's] conflict with Israel and the water flowing out of the rock is most marked and instructive, and in full keeping with the believer's conflict with his evil nature, which conflict is, as we know, consequent upon his having the new nature, and the Holy Ghost dwelling therein. Israel's conflict began when they stood in the full power of redemption, and had tasted "that spiritual meat and drunk of that spiritual Rock." Until they met Amalek, they had nothing to do. They did not cope with Pharaoh.... All the previous conflict had been between Jehovah and the enemy.... The Lord had fought for them; but now He fights in or by them.

Now it is when the Holy Ghost thus takes up His abode in us, consequent upon Christ's death and resurrection, that our conflict begins. Christ has fought for us; the Holy Ghost fights in us.[12]

Notice that God's children cannot fight this battle without God. When the Holy Spirit takes up residence in us, the battle for our soul (our mind, will, and emotions) begins. One of those warring parties within us is the flesh, the old man, trying to resurrect and maintain control over our soul. The other party is the indwelling presence of the Holy Spirit, our new nature, battling to keep the old man in the grave. This war is closely monitored by Jesus, who is seated at the right hand of the Father, making intercession for us. His intercession is constant and unchanging, but we can waver. As we keep our focus on Him through prayer (intimate fellowship with God) and the prayers of fellow believers, the new nature controls our soul. But as soon as we try to fight this battle by ourselves, the old man will gain control.

This proper focus on God is illustrated in Exodus 17:9-13. While the Israelites had to battle the Amalekites (the flesh) personally, God was not absent from the battle. God was battling for them through the raised hands of Moses. But notice that Moses was not alone and his hands were not empty. Aaron and Hur were there to strengthen Moses much like the prayers of others are there to strengthen us when we grow weary. Also, Moses held up the rod that represented the power of God so that all could see Who was fighting with them. Mackintosh expounds on this.

> We have, here, two distinct things, name-
> ly, conflict and intercession. Christ is on high for

us, while the Holy Ghost carries on the mighty struggle in us. The two things go together. It is as we enter, by faith, into the prevalency of Christ's intercession on our behalf, that we make head [way] against our evil nature. [So] there are [those] who seek to overlook the fact of the Christian's conflict with the flesh. They look upon regeneration as a total change or renewal of the old nature.... We are distinctly taught in the Word [however] that the believer carries about with him that which answers to Amalek, that is, "the flesh"—"the old man"– "the carnal mind...." In Romans 6 we read, "Let not sin therefore reign in your mortal bodies." Such a precept would be entirely uncalled for if the flesh were not existing in the believer. It would be out of character to tell us not to let sin reign, if it were not actually dwelling in us. There is a great difference between dwelling and reigning. It dwells in a believer, but it reigns in an unbeliever....

...Moses had the rod of God with him on the hill–the rod with which he had smitten the rock. This rod was the expression or symbol of the power of God, which is seen alike in atonement and intercession. When the work of atonement was accomplished, Christ took His seat in heaven, and sent down the Holy Ghost to take up His abode in the Church; so that there is an

inseparable connection between the work of
Christ and the work of the Spirit. There is the
application of the power of God in each.[13]

Many Christians believe upon Jesus Christ but deny
the power received through the baptism with the Holy
Spirit. But Jesus said, "…ye shall receive power, after
that the Holy Ghost is come upon you: and ye shall be
witnesses unto me both in Jerusalem, and in all Judaea
and in Samaria, and unto the uttermost part of the earth"
(Acts 1:8). Many Christians confess Jesus as their Lord,
but they do not surrender their flesh to the leadership
of the Holy Spirit. Without the work of both Jesus
Christ and the Holy Spirit, they are doubting, wavering
Christians that the world loves to use as their excuse for
not believing in Christ.

We are not just mere men upon receiving salvation
and becoming totally immersed (baptized) into the water
(the death and resurrection of Jesus Christ) and fire (the
power of the Holy Spirit). We are representatives of the
Most High God, Who loves to see His Son glorified in us
and through us. Praise the Lord!

Chapter Six

God Is Not Mocked

*Be not deceived; **God is not mocked:***
for whatsoever a man soweth, that shall he also reap.
Galatians 6:7

The Spiritual Wilderness VS the Spiritual Promised Land

To the surprise of many Christians, we are not
to be wandering (wondering) around in the spiritual
wilderness. We are to be living in the spiritual promised
land. And how do we get to that promised land? We get
there through the Word of God.

The Word of God clearly states all of His promises
to His children. We are to read, to study, to meditate,
and to believe God's Word. Then we are to act
according to His Word in order to live abundantly in
His promised land!

God showed me that the wilderness of New
Testament believers are those times when believers
allow doubt to overshadow and make ineffectual God's
Word and ways. We allow our thinking, so limited in
understanding, to darken the truth of God's Word. We
allow our thinking to override our knowledge of what

God says. God has a plan for each of us that can be undone by our wrong thinking, desires, and pursuits.

Many in the body of Christ have believed the lie that God leads us into the wilderness to teach, test, and train us. But remembering that the wilderness of today is the doubting mind of believers, ask yourself this, "Why would God lead us into areas filled with doubt and unbelief?" It goes against His Word. Jesus said,

> But when he, the Spirit of truth, comes, he will
> guide you into all truth. He will not speak on
> his own; he will speak only what he hears, and
> he will tell you what is yet to come.
> He will bring glory to me by taking from what
> is mine and making it known to you.
> All that belongs to the Father is mine. That is
> why I said the Spirit will take from what is
> mine and make it known to you.
> (John 16:13-15 NIV)

What a promise! The Holy Spirit leads and guides us into all truth. Jesus said nothing about the Holy Spirit leading us into the wilderness for a training seminar. Instead, the Holy Spirit is the One that teaches us by taking all that we have in Jesus and making it known to us. The Holy Spirit actively renews our mind–giving us the mind of Christ. But we cannot remain passive. We have a role to play. Our role is to study the Word and then make the decision to apply it properly to our daily lives.

Are you beginning to see that the promised land of the New Testament is the mind of Christ available to all believers? We only have to trust that God is faithful to His Word. As born again, spirit-filled believers, we no longer have to contend with the wilderness (the doubting mind) because the Holy Spirit is there to keep us, teach us, and guide us.

So, why is it Christians continue to have wilderness experiences? James tells us.

> If any of you lack wisdom, let him ask of God,
> that giveth to all *men* liberally, and upbraideth
> not; and it shall be given him.
> But let him ask in faith, nothing wavering. For
> he that wavereth is like a wave of the sea driven
> with the wind and tossed.
> For let not that man think that he shall receive
> any thing of the Lord.
> A double minded man *is* unstable in all his ways.
> (James 1:5-8)

We don't need anyone to help us wander into the wilderness. We do very well all by ourselves because of our thought life. Our doubting minds cause us to be unstable and unable to receive the promises of God.

So, is the Holy Spirit really the One Who leads us into this state of confusion and unrest? The answer is no. James tells us to ask for wisdom that leads us out of the wilderness, and God will give it to us generously.

Temptations of Satan

Immediately, after making these statements, many Christians will cite Bible passages clearly stating that the Holy Spirit led Jesus into the wilderness. And the reason for this was for Him to be tempted by Satan. Well, let us look at this more closely.

James 1:14 tells us "every man is tempted, when he is drawn away of his own lust, and enticed." James clearly states that our own lusts (due to the sin nature) draw us into temptation. Yet, as Matthew Henry explains, Jesus did not have a sin nature. Therefore, the Holy Spirit had to lead Jesus into the wilderness. While there, Jesus showed us the importance of fasting to crucify the flesh. Through prayer and fasting, Jesus overcame the tempter, Satan, for us. And because of Jesus' victory, we know how to have the same victory over all of Satan's temptations.[1]

John tells us specifically what those temptations are:

> Do not love *or* cherish the world or the things
> that are in the world. If anyone loves the world,
> love for the Father is not in him.
> For all that is in the world–**the lust of the flesh**
> [craving for sensual gratification] and **the lust of
> the eyes** [greedy longings of the mind] and **the
> pride of life** [assurance in one's own resources or
> in the stability of earthly things]–these do not come
> from the Father but are from the world [itself].
> (1 John 2:15-16 Amp, *emphasis mine*)

The lust of the flesh, the lust of the eyes, and the pride of life are the same temptations Satan used against Eve in the garden and against Jesus in the wilderness. His deceitful tactics never change. He is still using these three temptations against believers today.

In Genesis, Eve's first mistake was having a conversation with Satan. She was deceived, and she entertained the thoughts of Satan. After that, Eve allowed these *wrong thoughts* like seeds to take root in her heart that brought *wrong desires*. Finally, Eve along with Adam acted on those *wrong desires* that *gave birth to sin*. And sin brought death to man's spirit, soul, and body. God's law of sowing and reaping is always in effect even when the seed and the crop are ungodly (See Genesis 8:22).

> And the serpent said unto the woman, Ye shall not surely die:
> For God doth know that in the day ye eat thereof, then your eyes shall be opened, and ye shall be as gods, knowing good and evil.
> And when the woman saw that the tree *was* good for food, and that it *was* pleasant to the eyes, and a tree to be desired to make *one* wise, she took of the fruit thereof, and did eat, and gave also unto her husband with her; and he did eat.
> (Genesis 3:4-6)

We see the three areas in which Satan tempted Eve. First, Satan told Eve she would not die from eating of the tree of the knowledge of good and evil. So, Eve looked on the forbidden fruit and determined the fruit was "good for food." (The first temptation was *the lust of the flesh* in which *the body* craved immediate gratification of its senses.)

Then, Satan suggested that the fruit would open the eyes of her understanding. Therefore, the more Eve continued to look upon the forbidden fruit, the more she desired it based on her emotions. She made a decision based on outward appearance that the forbidden fruit was not only "good for food" but also that the fruit was "pleasant." (The second temptation was *the lust of the eyes* in which *the soul–mind, will, and emotions*–were assaulted).

Finally, because Eve chose not to close her eyes and ears to wrong thinking, she believed Satan's lie that eating the fruit would make them "as gods, knowing good and evil." The sin of pride caused her to believe that somehow God was withholding some good and precious gift from her, so she took matters into her own hands by taking and eating the fruit. (The last temptation was *the pride of life* in which *the spirit* once committed only to God became self-interested.)

Matthew Henry observed that the desire for knowledge (often thought to be wisdom) leads to destruction.[2] Adam and Eve did not realize that God had equipped them with all they needed to know to live their lives in abundance. Both Adam and Eve fell into sin as a result of exerting their self-will. Their hearts had become hardened through unbelief in God's Word, and they took and ate the forbidden fruit.

James writes:

> Let no man say when he is tempted, I am
> tempted of God: for God cannot be tempted
> with evil, neither tempteth he any man:
> But every man is tempted, when he is drawn
> away of his own lust, and enticed.
> Then when lust hath conceived, it bringeth forth sin:
> and sin, when it is finished, bringeth forth death.
> (James 1:13-15)

James makes it clear that the sin is not in having wrong thoughts. Satan is the father of lies, and he is the author of wrong thoughts. We have to choose what we do with wrong thoughts so that those thoughts do not lead us into sin. We are to cast out the wrong thoughts by replacing them with what God says (See 2 Corinthians 10:5).

In Matthew 4, we read how Jesus soundly defeated Satan when Satan brought temptations (wrong thoughts) against Jesus' body, soul, and spirit. Just as Satan had with Eve, He tried to engage Jesus in a conversation by saying, "If thou be the Son of God…" And just as with Eve, Satan tried to cause Jesus to doubt Who He was and to question His relationship with God.

What did Jesus say to this? Nothing! He knew exactly Who He is. Just like Jesus, every believer must be fully persuaded who he or she is in Jesus Christ (See Appendix B: In Christ Jesus). We are blood-bought, brothers and sisters of Jesus and sons and daughters of the Most High God.

As we continue in Matthew 4, we read that Satan tempted Jesus with the lust of the flesh–an attack on His body. Jesus was starving after a forty-day fast, and Satan tempted Him to abuse God's power by turning stones into bread. Jesus had already committed His body to God at the River Jordan. Jesus was already fully persuaded that God alone was His provider. So, rather than engage Satan in an argument, Jesus responded with the only offensive weapon in His armor–the Word of God (See Ephesians 6:17). "It is written, Man shall not live by bread alone, but by every word that proceedeth out of the mouth of God" (Matthew 4:4).

Satan's next assault was on Jesus' soul. Satan placed Jesus on the pinnacle of the temple in the holy city and said, "Jump." Then he misrepresented Psalm 91:11 and 12 that promises God's protection from harm.

Psalm says,

> For he shall give his angels charge over thee, to keep thee in all thy ways.
> They shall bear thee up in *their* hands, lest thou dash thy foot against a stone.
> (Psalm 91:11-12)

Satan misquoted,

> And saith unto him, If thou be the Son of God, cast thyself down: for it is written, He shall give his angels charge concerning thee: and in *their*

hands they shall bear thee up, lest at any time
thou dash thy foot against a stone.
(Matthew 4:6)

Satan deceptively omitted the phrase "to keep thee
in all thy ways" because he knows that angels keep us
when we are walking in God's ways not in our ways.[3]
Also, Satan added the words "at any time" to imply that
we can merrily go our own way and still expect God to
fulfill His promise of protection.

Please, do not misunderstand. I am not saying God
lifts His hand of protection to teach us a lesson. On the
contrary, we choose to walk out from under His umbrella
of protection by our own lusts. Remember, angels go to
work for us based on God's Word alone.

This lust of the eyes was designed to tempt Jesus
into greedily longing, demanding, and manipulating
the letter of God's Word. Satan revels in reducing the
Word of God to just an intellectual pursuit which in turn
keeps the knowledge, understanding, and wisdom of it
hidden. This self-centered approach to God's Word stops
the promised blessings of God due to wrong motives.
Glorifying "self" rather than glorifying God was the
reason Jesus often called the religious leaders hypocrites.

This second temptation gives us insight into
Satan's evil device of twisting Scripture to achieve his
evil purpose. Jesus knew that using God's Word and
power wrongly just to receive the accolades of men was
sinning against God.

Jesus had committed His soul (mind, will, and emotions) to God in the Jordan River forty days earlier. If God wanted to place Him on that pinnacle–fine. If God wanted to place Him on a cross–fine. Jesus already desired what God desired. Satan was unable to plant seeds of wrong thoughts about God's will to sprout wrong desires of self-will. No, Jesus understood the Spirit of God's Word that prompted this reply. "It is written again, Thou shalt not tempt the Lord thy God" (Matthew 4:7).

The last temptation, the pride of life, was the most heinous. This attack was directed at Jesus' spirit. Satan took Jesus to an extremely high mountaintop and supernaturally showed Him all the kingdoms of the world in all their glory. Jesus was told that all the authority, power, and riches of the world could be His for the price of falling down and worshipping Satan.

This repulsive proposal caused Jesus to respond, "Get thee hence, Satan: for it is written. Thou shalt worship the Lord thy God, and him only shalt thou serve" (Matthew 4:10). Jesus had committed His spirit, soul, and body to God at the Jordan. He did not waver in knowing by Whose authority, power, and provision He would rely on to conduct Himself for the next three years. And He had no doubt who would be soundly defeated in the end. Satan had nothing that Jesus needed or wanted, especially a counterfeit god.

The Word of God and the power of the Holy Spirit forced Satan to retreat like a whipped dog. We are told later that Satan had nothing in Jesus (See John 14:30), and we, as believers, can attain that same state. With the authority of Jesus' name, the proper application of His Word, and the power of the Holy Spirit, we can enforce Jesus' victory over temptations.

We have to stop allowing Satan to lead us back into the wilderness of doubt, unbelief, and disobedience. If we renew our minds through the Word as the Spirit leads us, we can live in the promised land where all the blessings of God are abundantly given.

The Wilderness–Fear Due to Doubt

In the King James Version of the Bible, the word *wilderness* appears 270 times in the Old Testament but only 35 times in the New Testament. And not once in the New Testament is the word *wilderness* used in reference to new covenant believers under the dispensation of grace.

So, why is it that the wilderness is spoken of so often in the Old Testament but relatively few times in the New Testament? Could it be that Jesus came to earth and whooped Satan and his demons?

For in Christ all the fullness of the Deity lives in bodily form,
And you have been given fullness in Christ,
who is the head over every power and authority.
In him you were also circumcised, in the putting off of the sinful nature, not with a circumcision done by the hands of men but with the

circumcision done by Christ,

Having been buried with him in baptism and
raised with him through your faith in the
power of God, who raised him from the dead.
When you were dead in your sins and in the
uncircumcision of your sinful nature, God made
you alive with Christ. **He forgave us all our sins,
Having canceled the written code, with its regulations, that was against us and that stood opposed
to us; he took it away, nailing it to the cross.
And having disarmed the powers and authorities, he made a public spectacle of them,
triumphing over them by the cross.**
(Colossians 2:9-15 NIV, *emphasis mine*)

This Scripture should make us rejoice and praise
God! So, why is it that so many Christians missed the
memo? The memo being: *The war is won; now occupy the
promised land until Jesus returns.* I believe the cause stems
from many years of wrong teaching.

Let us look at the wilderness more closely. The
wilderness is often used in the Bible as a noun meaning
"an uninhabited region"[4] or as an adjective signifying
"solitary, lonely, desolate, uninhabited."[5] Hey, let's face it;
if we are experiencing the wilderness, we are in a desert
wasteland. Now, does that sound like the promises of
God? The answer is no!

The wilderness is a place of barely enough. It
abounds in fear of lack, in constant crisis, in murmuring

and complaining, in no peace, and in no joy. If you don't believe me, read Exodus through Deuteronomy. You will read about an entire generation of Israelites dying in the wilderness because of their hardened hearts that always doubted, questioned, disputed, reasoned, argued, and debated the very character and nature of God.

Many Christians today are suffering in the wilderness because they do not understand that Satan is the one who has led them into lack. God, Who is faithful, is with them in the wilderness. He is there to provide the necessary miracles to keep Christians much like He did with the Israelites through the miracle provision of food, water, and clothing. But God's plan for Christians is not the wilderness. How could it be in light of the finished work of His Son?

I am not against miracles. I have needed God's miraculous work in my life, too. Miracles are often, however, preceded by crisis. I do not believe God's best for His children is to live from miracle to miracle (crisis to crisis) like the Israelites. God wants us to be living from blessing to blessing. And God's blessing is grace, God's unmerited, super-abundant favor through Jesus Christ.

> But if God so clothes the grass of the field,
> which today is alive *and* green and tomorrow is
> tossed into the furnace, will He not much more
> surely clothe you, O you of little faith?
> Therefore do not worry *and* be anxious, saying,
> What are we going to have to eat? or, What are

we going to have to drink? or, What are we going to have to wear?

For the Gentiles (heathen) wish for *and*
crave *and* diligently seek all these things,
and your heavenly Father knows well that
you need them all.

**But seek (aim at and strive after) first of
all His kingdom and His righteousness
(His way of doing and being right), and
then all these things taken together will be
given you besides.**

(Matthew 6:30-33 Amp, *emphasis mine*)

Read what Jesus said as He personally invites us
into the promised land.

Come unto me, all *ye* that labour and are heavy
laden, and I will give you rest.

Take my yoke upon you, and learn of me; for I
am meek and lowly in heart: and ye shall find
rest unto your souls.

For my yoke *is* easy, and my burden is light.
(Matthew 11:28-30)

In Hebrews, we are told how to remain in the
promised land once we find rest in Jesus and take upon
us His easy yoke. Also, we are warned to take our lessons
from the Israelites' failures, so we do not take wrong
paths that lead us into the wilderness.

For we are made partakers of Christ, **if we
hold the beginning of our confidence** stedfast
unto the end;
While it is said, Today if ye will hear his voice,
harden not your hearts, as in the provocation.
For some, when they had heard, did pro-
voke: howbeit not all that came out of Egypt
by Moses.
But with whom was he grieved forty years? *was
it* not with them that had sinned, whose car-
cases fell in the wilderness?
And to whom sware he that they should not enter into his rest, but to them that believed not?
**So we see that they could not enter in because
of unbelief.**
(Hebrews 3:14-19, *emphasis mine*)

Doubting God's character and nature is what keeps
us from living free in the promised land and keeps us
in bondage to Satan. He has no rights to us once we
are blood-bought, children of God. That does not mean
he will not try to deceive us in order to keep us out of
the promised land. We have to take the faith (being
fully persuaded) that God has given every believer and
combine it with a steadfast belief (recognizing a fact or a
truth beyond the physical or soulish realm).

But without faith *it is* impossible to please *him*:
for he that cometh to God must believe that

he is, and *that* he is a rewarder of them that
diligently seek him.
(Hebrews 11:6)

The Promised Land–Faith Due to Belief

In the King James Version of the Bible, the
word *faith* appears in the Old Testament only two
times. But in the New Testament the word *faith*
appears 145 times.

So, why is the word *faith* used so often in the New
Testament but only twice in the Old Testament? Could
it be that Jesus paid the price for all to enter into the
inheritance of the blessing of grace by faith in Him?
Faith must have an object, and for Christians that object
is Jesus, plus nothing else. The covenant of grace that
God has made with the world can only be obtained
through Jesus. No matter how good or moral someone
is, everyone is born with a sin nature and has fallen
short of God's glory. But if we believe that Jesus is the
way to a right relationship with our heavenly Father,
then, by faith, we can enter into the finished work of
Jesus. His victory over Satan becomes our victory, too.
Because we accept the exchanged life of Jesus through
the saving faith of God, we can learn Who God is
personally, and experience all of His blessed grace. As
we grow in the knowledge of Him, we can have more
of the promised land manifested in our lives and less
wilderness living!

So, what is faith? The Bible says,

> NOW FAITH is the substance of things hoped
> for, the evidence of things not seen.
> (Hebrews 11:1)

> NOW FAITH is the assurance (the confirma-
> tion, the title deed) of the things [we] hope for,
> being the proof of things [we] do not see *and* the
> conviction of their reality [faith perceiving as
> real fact what is not revealed to the senses].
> (Hebrews 11:1 Amp)

> NOW FAITH is being sure of what we hope for
> and certain of what we do not see.
> (Hebrews 11:1 NIV)

Faith is a substance, an assurance, a confirmation, and a title deed to the something hoped for in God's promises. Okay, then *no* faith means *no* substance, *no* assurance, *no* confirmation, and *no* legal right to something hoped for in God's promises.

Faith is also the evidence, conviction, proof, and certainty of having that something from God's promises even though it remains unseen or not yet a reality in the physical realm. Therefore, *no* faith means: *no* evidence, *no* conviction, *no* proof, and *no* certainty of having that something from God's promises seen or made a reality in the physical realm.

Do you see how a Christian can live in either the promised land of God or the wilderness? We are the ones who decide where we live depending on whether we mix our faith with belief or doubt.

This should be encouraging to all believers because this means that big faith or small faith is not the issue. The issue is how much belief or unbelief we mix with our faith. Belief or unbelief determines how much of one's faith in the finished work of Jesus becomes manifested in the physical realm. Peter tells us,

> Grace and peace be multiplied unto you **through the knowledge of God, and of Jesus our Lord,**
> **According as his divine power hath given unto us all things that pertain unto life and godliness, through the knowledge of him that hath called us to glory and virtue:**
> Whereby are given unto us **exceeding great and precious promises: that by these ye might be partakers of the divine nature, having escaped the corruption that is in the world through lust.**
> (2 Peter 1:2-4, *emphasis mine*)

The previous Scripture is cause for celebration! We are told that we can take part in His nature and receive the manifestation of His promises by knowing

Him personally and intimately. Remember what Hebrews 11:6 tells us. We are the ones who have to come to Him. We must believe that He is, and we must believe that He is a rewarder of those who diligently seek Him. How do we do this? We do this by studying, meditating, and doing His Word His way (See 2 Timothy 3:16-17).

The Right Path

The difference between the wilderness and the promised land is easy to see. The wilderness is filled with lack; whereas, the promised land is filled with abundance. They are two completely different paths. The wilderness can be seen like this. "The way of the wicked is as darkness: they know not at what they stumble" (Proverbs 4:19). The promised land is just the opposite. "But the path of the just is as the shining light, that shineth more and more unto the perfect day" (Proverbs 4:18).

Many in the body of Christ are not seeing their path become brighter each day with the fullness of Christ's glory. Far too many Christians, who truly love God, are still walking in the paths of darkness in the world. They have not come to know God intimately nor shared in His glory that enables us to live more in His light. Consequently, the world cannot see the difference between themselves and many of the Christians they meet. Hence, many in the world do not see the need for the saving grace of Jesus Christ.

For those Christians who are on God's paths of righteousness, however, the world is drawn to them. They are drawn to the light that has not been hidden under a bushel basket. The light (the life) of Christ is manifested in these Christians that causes the world to stop and take notice. Jesus said, "...I am the light of the world: he that followeth me shall not walk in darkness, but shall have the light of life" (John 8:12).

But in the very next verse, who took issue with Jesus' remarks? The Pharisees told Jesus that He was lying about Who He is. The Pharisees and Sadducees (the religious leaders of that day) were the ones keeping the letter of the law in their own self-righteousness. Even today, some Christians claim to know the truth of God's Word but will criticize other Christians who are seeing the Word of God manifested in their lives in the form of His blessings. They claim the letter of the law but miss the Spirit of God's Word. Many either do not know or do not believe that we have the authority to use the name of Jesus Christ and have the right to place a demand on the anointing through the Holy Spirit. Some even sneer at this truth and hiss the words, "faith movement."

How can it be anything other than faith? We receive by faith! We are saved by grace through faith. And we stay on the path to the promised land by faith.

The promised land is for all who diligently seek to know God through learning the truth of His word. Many Christians recite God's Word with no effect. But those who come to know the truth of God's Word are being transformed into the image of Jesus Christ from glory to glory.

In a vision, God showed me believers' various levels of understanding with regard to His Word. I saw something that looked like the Grand Canyon. I watched as many people walked over the edge of the canyon not seeing the danger. Then, I saw others standing at the edge looking hopelessly across the great gulf of the canyon. Finally, I saw some that were walking across a bridge. I could *not* see the end of the bridge, but I believed that it spanned the entire width of the canyon. At the entrance of the bridge, I saw many people that seemed afraid to step onto the bridge. They were screaming franticly at those on the bridge to come back. It occurred to me that their terror was due to their inability to see the bridge.

As I asked the Holy Spirit for the meaning of this vision, He told me that the people walking over the edge of the canyon were deceived by false religion. They were unsaved.

The ones standing at the edge of the canyon looking out over the great gulf were saved. But they had no knowledge or understanding of what they had in Christ. They remained wandering in the wilderness just short of falling into the canyon.

As for those on the bridge, God reminded me of something I once heard concerning Peter's walk on the water. Jesus was walking on the water above all the turmoil of a violent sea. Peter asked Jesus to bid him to "come," and Jesus did. So, Peter stepped out of the boat and walked on Jesus' word: C – O – M - E. Once Peter ran out of Jesus' word, he began to sink.

The Holy Spirit showed me that the bridge over this great canyon was made from God's Word that was leading them to the promised land. Faith was required to step forward on the bridge because the bridge was being formed under their feet with each step.

As for the terrified saved on the wilderness side, they could not see the bridge because they had no faith in God's Word. They may have known the Word of God to recite it to others, but they did not have the understanding or wisdom to properly apply it. So they were unable to go across the bridge to the promised land.

What God was showing me was the difference in the two paths. "The way of the wicked *is* as darkness: they know not at what they stumble" (Proverbs 4:19). "But the path of the just *is* as the shining light, that shineth more and more unto the perfect day" (Proverbs 4:18).

The Importance of God's Word

Christians have been given the most precious gift in the form of our Lord and Savior, Jesus Christ. According to John 1, we know that Jesus is the very Word of God made flesh. He is the true light of the world, through which grace (unearned, undeserved favor and spiritual blessing) and truth come. In 1 John 1, we are told that Jesus Christ is eternal life. And eternal life is defined as the ability for a born-again, spirit-filled child of God, "...to know (to perceive, recognize, become acquainted with, and understand) You, the only true and real God, and [likewise] to know Him, Jesus [as the] Christ (the Anointed One, the Messiah), Whom You have sent" (John 17:3 Amp).

Eternal life is ours by believing on Jesus Christ as our Savior. Many upon salvation, however, do not find out what they have in Christ. Therefore, they continue in the path of the wicked. They are saved but never grow into what God has purposed for them. They continue in doubt and stumble in darkness on a destructive path. Many fail to believe that God has the promised land available for them now.

They remain confused about Who God truly is and question His character and nature by doubting His love for them. When bad things continue to happen in the realm of "sin, sickness/disease, poverty, bad habits, lack of spiritual power, and failure in prayer,"[6] they will quote portions of Scripture that seemingly prove that God's will cannot be known. As a result, they end their doubt-filled prayers with "if it be thy will." One misinterpreted Scripture they often use to comfort themselves is this,

> For my thoughts *are* not your thoughts, neither
> *are* your ways my ways, saith the LORD.
> For *as* the heavens are higher than the earth, so
> are my ways higher than your ways, and my
> thoughts than your thoughts.
> (Isaiah 55:8-9)

What people fail to study are the verses that come before and after verses 8 and 9. "Let the wicked forsake his way, and the unrighteous man his thoughts: and let him return unto the LORD, and he will have mercy upon him; and to our God, for he will abundantly pardon" (Isaiah 55:7). Clearly, verse 7 is addressing unrighteous individuals, but I dare say it could also be applied to righteous individuals who have not renewed their minds to who they are as new creations in Christ. These people, through ignorance or choice, decide not to know God's thoughts and ways. They continue to walk in the world of darkness by the enticements of Satan through the lust of flesh, the lust of the eyes, and the pride of life.

In Isaiah 55, God is instructing the unrighteous (the wicked). He is encouraging them to draw near so that He can impart to them His thoughts and ways. Read His promise to them in the verses that follow verses 8 and 9.

> For as the rain cometh down, and the snow
> from heaven, and returneth not thither, but
> watereth the earth, and maketh it bring forth
> and bud, that it may give seed to the sower, and
> bread to the eater:
> So shall my word be that goeth forth out of my
> mouth: it shall not return unto me void, but
> it shall accomplish that which I please, and it
> shall prosper *in the thing* whereto I sent it.
> (Isaiah 55:10-11)

We can see this law of sowing and reaping at work both naturally and spiritually. And Who set up this law? God, Himself, is the One Who spoke it. Just as He made snow and rain to water the earth and bring forth what man needs to live, the same is true for His Word. In nature we see seedtime and harvest easily. But when it comes to the Word of God, many seem completely unaware of this law. The Word of God must be received into our hearts through study and watered through meditation. Then we must patiently let the Word germinate and grow through the guiding, teaching, and comforting of the Holy Spirit. Our unwavering faith and belief in God's Word will bring forth a crop for harvest.

God, Himself, spoke and now He expects us to speak His Word back to Him in faith. Then He promises that He will act on it and have it accomplish whatever He sent it to accomplish.

> And this is the confidence that we have in him,
> that, if we ask any thing according to his will,
> he heareth us:
> And if we know that he hears us, whatsoever
> we ask, we know that we have the petitions that
> we desired of him.
> (1 John 5:14-15)

This previous Scripture tells us to speak what God has spoken and to believe that He will fulfill His Word. Just speaking His Word without faith is not enough.

Then it is just positive confession. No, our speaking God's Word in faith is based on what we believe Jesus accomplished through His work on the cross, through the power that resurrected Him from the dead, and through the authority of His name. Our confidence in Jesus causes all things that can be named to bow.

> ...Let us lay aside every weight, and the sin
> which doth so easily beset *us*, and let us run
> with patience the race that is set before us.
> Looking unto Jesus the author and finisher of
> *our* faith; who for the joy that was set before
> him endured the cross, despising the shame,
> and is set down at the right hand of the
> throne of God.
> (Hebrews 12:1-2)

When we begin to diligently seek God through His Word, we will realize that in Christ Jesus we have been given everything. Once we see that truth, the knowledge of it will bring the understanding and wisdom that makes His Word, "quick and powerful, and sharper than any two-edged sword, piercing even to the dividing asunder of soul and spirit, and of the joints and marrow, and is a discerner of the thoughts and intents of the heart" (Hebrews 4:12). When we sow His Word into our hearts, we will begin to experience harvest in the form of new thoughts (the mind of Christ), new behaviors (Christ-like behaviors), a healed body, prosperity, and the manifestation of answered prayers by the power of the Holy Spirit.

Why is God not mocked? God has told us why–the law of sowing and reaping. Whatever we sow, we will reap. If we sow His Word, He is faithful to bring forth the intended manifestation.

> For as the rain cometh down, and the snow
> from heaven, and returneth not thither, but
> watereth the earth, and maketh it bring forth
> and bud, that it may give seed to the sower, and
> bread to the eater:
> So shall my word be that goeth forth out of my
> mouth: it shall not return unto me void, but
> it shall accomplish that which I please, and it
> shall prosper *in the thing* whereto I sent it.
> (Isaiah 55:10-11)

Lessons from the Israelites:
The Israelites Passed through Many Lands

Once again, C. H. Mackintosh's commentary helps us to see powerful revelations for the modern day church through the experiences of the Israelites. One such revelation is the spiritual meaning in the various places the Israelites lived in throughout the Old Testament: Egypt, the Wilderness, Canaan, and Babylon.

Mackintosh describes Egypt as a "moral desert"[7] of the world. He states that Egypt represents the world where our flesh resides. Our flesh will ever crave natural surroundings. Our bodies live in the world in which our five senses scream for those things it believes will make it happy. The flesh is constantly telling the soul (mind, will, and emotions) that if it feels good, then do it. Christians must recognize that the cost of their uncontrolled flesh will be more than they want to pay.

As mentioned earlier, the wilderness of the Israelites is representative of the believer's doubting mind. Doubt and unbelief in God kept the Israelites in the wilderness for forty years longer than they needed to be, and doubt and unbelief will keep a believer in a spiritual wasteland in much the same way. The soul (the mind, will, and emotions) of a believer is truly stupid. It will do what either one's flesh or one's born-again spirit tells it to do. The soul is constantly wavering between the two until a believer makes a decisive decision to follow after God with all his or her heart.

The land of Canaan, the land of promise for the Israelites, represents our born-again spirit being continually filled with the life of Christ. Through the power of the Holy Spirit, we are able to receive all the promises of God as we become intimately acquainted with His Word and His ways. Intimacy with God enables us to enter into His spiritual promised land. The mind of Christ enables us to live in God's promised land, but the doubting mind keeps us living in the wilderness. Notice that the soul is what the Holy Spirit and the flesh are warring to possess in a believer.

Apparently, these three lands that the Israelites passed through are directly related to our tri-part being: Egypt, the world where the flesh lives; the wilderness, the soul; and Canaan, the reborn spirit. Ultimately, each influences our spiritual walk with God. But Mackintosh mentioned a fourth land, Babylon, that also played a significant role in the Israelites' history.

> There is a wide moral difference between Egypt and Babylon, which it is important to understand. Egypt was that out of which Israel came; Babylon was that into which they were afterwards carried. (Compare Amos 5:25-27 with Acts 7:42-43) Egypt expresses what man

has made of the world; Babylon expresses what Satan has made, is making, or will make, of the professing Church. Hence, we are not only surrounded with the circumstances of Egypt, but also by the moral principles of Babylon....

The "power" of the Holy Ghost will necessarily produce, or express itself in a certain "form, and the enemy's aim has ever been to rob the professing church of the power, while he leads her to cling to, and perpetuate the form–to stereotype the form when all the spirit and life has passed away. Thus he builds the spiritual Babylon. The stones of which this city is built are lifeless professors; and the slime or mortar which binds these stones together is a form of godliness without the power."[8]

This describes many who are in the church today. I longed for years to be delivered from my destructive life, but what I saw of the church made me run from God. Not until I met a spirit-filled believer did my opinion of God and the church change. I saw the power of God operate in her life in the form of answered prayers because this woman confidently trusted in God and His love. Through her love of God and her love of others, I came to know a loving, caring, and "more than enough" God Who worked in my life to deliver me from spiritual death, depression, loneliness, sickness, and debt.

I am intimately acquainted with all the lands that the Israelites passed through. I lived forty years in Egypt (the world), and without the daily renewal of my mind, my flesh would gladly return. I have had the wilderness experiences (the doubting mind) after I think I do not have to spend the necessary time with God. I am amazed at how quickly my heart hardens toward God. I have visited Babylon when I attend churches in which those in attendance practice the form of godliness but deny His power. But I have been to the promised land also. This land is rich with the blessings of God, and I desire to make it my home.

So, why are we, as Christians, not going in and taking possession of the promised land? Mackintosh explains that we are like the spies that went into Canaan. We do not fully believe the words God spoke through Moses. "Behold, the LORD thy God hath set the land before thee: go up *and* possess *it*, as the LORD God of thy fathers hath said unto thee; fear not, neither be discouraged" (Deuteronomy 1:21).

Now I know, as did Mackintosh, what God spoke in Numbers.

> AND THE LORD spake unto Moses, saying,
> Send thou men, that they may search the land
> of Canaan, which I give unto the children of Is-
> rael: of every tribe of their fathers shall ye send
> a man, every one a ruler among them.
> (Numbers 13:1-2)

But do not neglect what is spoken in Deuteronomy. After God told the Israelites to go and take the land He had given them, the Israelites decided they wanted spies to go in first. Moses recounts what actually happened.

> Behold, the LORD thy God hath set the land before thee: go up *and* possess *it,* as the LORD God of thy fathers hath said unto thee; fear not, neither be discouraged.
> **And ye came near unto me every one of you, and said**, We will send men before us, and they shall search us out the land, and bring us word again by what way we must go up, and into what cities we shall come.
> (Deuteronomy 1:21-22, *emphasis mine*)

Mackintosh explains,

> The Lord their God had given them the land, and set it before them. It was theirs by His free gift, the gift of His sovereign grace, in pursuance of the covenant made with their fathers. It was His eternal purpose to possess the land of Canaan through the seed of Abraham His friend. This ought to have been enough to set their hearts perfectly at rest, not only as to the character of the land, but also as to their entrance upon it. There was no need of spies. Faith never wants to spy what God has given.

It argues that what He has given must be worth having; and that he is able to put us in full possession of all that His grace has bestowed.

So faith would have reasoned; for it always reasons from God down to circumstances; never from circumstances up to God. "If God be for us, who can be against us?" This is faith's argument, grand in its simplicity, and simple in its moral grandeur.... Faith exults in seeing God triumphing over difficulties.

True it is that, in the history given in Numbers, the Lord told Moses to send the spies. But why? Because of the moral condition of the people. And here we see the characteristic difference and yet the lovely harmony of the two books. Numbers gives us the public history, Deuteronomy the secret source of the mission of the spies;...

It may be, however, that the reader still feels some difficulty in reference to the question of the spies. He may feel disposed to ask, how it could be wrong to send them, when the Lord told them to do so? The answer is, the wrong was not in the act of sending them when they were told, but in the wish to send them at all. The wish was the fruit of unbelief; and the command to send them was because of that unbelief.[9]

So, in answer to the question, why are Christians not going in to possess the land? The answer is unbelief.

Consequently, Christians tend to live in God's permissive will more than His perfect will. God allowed the Israelites to send in spies due to His permissive will, but His perfect will was for them just to believe and go in and possess His promised land.

Mackintosh points out two other instances from the Bible in which God's permissive will and perfect will can be seen. In Matthew 19, Jesus explains that divorce was never God's will for man, but because of man's hardness of heart, He permitted Moses to make allowances for divorce in the law.

Another example of God's permissive will versus His perfect will was in God permitting kings to reign over Israel. God's perfect will was that He alone rule over Israel. Yet, He allowed Israel to be ruled by kings that led them to disaster.

Throughout the Bible, God's perfect will is doubted, and God allows man to live in His permissive will. When will we learn that God's perfect will is our perfect will? When will we learn that God is love? When will we learn that God is for us not against us?

We will learn all these things as we make a decision to trust Him. And we can only trust Him if we know Him! That means we play a significant role in God's purpose and plan. Please, do not misunderstand. God will get done on earth what He wants to accomplish. It just will not be through doubting, wavering believers.

Mackintosh testifies for pages about the importance of faith. Faith without doubting:

...draws down power and blessing, not
only for ourselves but for others." "Faith is
the divine secret of the whole matter, the main
spring of Christian life, from first to last." "Faith
wavers not, staggers not." "Faith puts us into
direct contact with the eternal spring of love in
God Himself; and the necessary consequence
is that our hearts are drawn out in love to all
who belong to Him—all in whom we can, in the
very feeblest way, trace His blessed image."
"In short, there is no limit to the blessing which
we might enjoy at the hand of our God, if our
hearts were more governed by that simple faith
which ever counts on Him, and which He ever
delights to honour.[10]

The Bible tells us the only time Jesus could not do
mighty works was due to the unbelief of the people (See
Matthew 13:57-58). Yet, many times, He tells others they
were made whole according to "their" faith. Let this be
the proof we need that God desires us to possess the land
by faith free from doubt and unbelief.

How can we have faith that is free from doubt and
unbelief? Faith comes by hearing and hearing by the
Word of God (See Romans 10:7). Doubt and unbelief
leave by feeding on God's Word. Therefore, studying
God's Word for ourselves by the power of the Holy
Spirit is imperative to finding out what He has truly said
(the promised land). Guard your heart against Egypt

(the world) and Babylon (the form of godliness without power) so that you do not have any more wilderness experiences (the doubting mind).

God is not mocked. We reap what we sow. If we continue to sow doubt into hardened heart soil, we will reap the crop of "barely enough" in the wilderness or "less than enough" in the land of Babylon. But if we sow faith through belief in His Word into well-fertilized heart soil, we will reap an abundant crop of "blessing" as we live peacefully in His promised land. But keep in mind that His blessing is His grace through Jesus Christ's finished work combined with the work of the Holy Spirit that enables us to have the manifestations here on earth. And those manifestations (His glory) will make others draw near to Him, also.

Chapter Seven

God Is Not the Author of Confusion

*For **God is not the author of confusion**,*
but of peace, as in all churches of the saints.
1 Corinthians 14:33

Why are Christians Defeated?

When I encounter Christians who lack confidence in receiving from God, I find that very few of them spend much time reading, studying, and meditating on God's Word. And for those Christians who do spend time in God's Word, their lack of receiving from God may be attributed to not allowing the Holy Spirit to reveal the truth of His Word.

These Christians justify their lack by reasoning that God is withholding from them for some unknown divine purpose. They will use phrases like "God is sovereign" and "you can never know what He will do." Typically, this thinking will lead them to end their prayers with "if it be thy will."

Lack of knowledge of God's true nature and character causes Christians to speak this way about God. They have believed some religious notion of God, but they do not know Him personally–intimately. They have *not* allowed His Spirit through revelation knowledge of His Word to bring them into a close personal relationship and fellowship with their heavenly Father. If they really knew Him, they would know that through Jesus we have a better covenant with better promises (See Hebrews 8:6). We do not have to wait for the "sweet by and by" to receive what God has for us; we have eternal life now.

Many Christians, who have suffered defeat, often use the book of Job to support their position that God is the reason they are not free from the problems of this world. But Job is really an account of one who learned how to overcome evil through a better understanding of Who God truly is.

Well, What about Job?

My mother tells me that when I was young, I was notorious for telling the ending of books and movies. Oh, how people would get upset with me. But in the case of the book of Job, please read the ending first and tell everyone about it. At the end of Job, he is completely healed and given back twice what was stolen from him.

Notice Job's family, health, wealth, and reputation were stolen. And we are told who did it. Satan was the one who stole Job's possessions, killed his children, and destroyed his health and relationships. Doesn't this confirm John 10:10 that tells us that Satan is the one who steals, kills, and destroys?

So many focus on what Satan was able to do to Job, but they fail to see what God was able to do for Job once Job listened to Him. After Job understood that he had based his belief on faulty knowledge about God, he stopped blaming God and stopped promoting his own self-righteousness. Then he was able to submit to God, resist the devil, and see the devil flee.

I asked God once what I could say to those who want to use Job as their banner for remaining in defeat. The Holy Spirit revealed that the lessons to be learned from Job are that God is faithful; He is willing to reveal His true nature; and He is exceedingly patient with us even when we blame Him for what the devil is doing. Also, He showed me that Job's lack of knowledge bound him, but the revelation knowledge of God's nature and character set Job free.

In chapters one and two of Job, it is often taught that God gave Satan permission to steal, kill, and destroy. God said to Satan, "…Have you considered My servant Job, that there is none like him on the earth, a blameless and upright man, one who [reverently] fears God and abstains from *and* shuns evil [because it is wrong]?" (Job 1:8 Amp).

What is God actually saying to Satan as God describes Job? God was not inviting Satan to take his best shot at Job because Job was without sin. God was saying that Job had met God's standard for being called righteous in God's eyes. Job by faith had reverential fear and awe of God–the beginning of wisdom (See Proverbs 9:10). This wisdom caused Job to turn from evil (See Proverbs 8:13). As a result, God's grace (unmerited favor) was manifested in Job's life.

For this reason Satan said, "Have you not put a hedge of protection about him and his house and all that he has, on every side? You have conferred prosperity *and* happiness upon him in the work of his hands, and his possessions have increased in the land" (Job 1:10 Amp). Sounds much like the blessing of Abraham. God accounted Job's faith in Him as righteousness, and the blessing of God (grace) came upon Job.

Religious teaching has perversely interpreted events in Job. Many believe that God treated Job much like the gods in Greek mythology treated their human subjects. No, this is *not* our God's nature. Read the conversation God and Satan had before verse 8, "And the LORD said to Satan, From where did you come? Then Satan answered the LORD, From going to and fro on the earth and from walking up and down on it" (Job 1:7 Amp).

We know from Scripture why Satan walks about the earth. He is seeking someone to devour (See 1 Peter 5:8). Satan searches for someone like Job, who even though was counted righteous, had allowed fear to let down God's hedge of protection. Job admitted, "For the thing which I greatly feared is come upon me, and that which I was afraid of is come unto me" (Job 3:25).

Fear, which is faith in Satan's lies, was an invitation for Satan to wreak havoc. The following Scripture confirms this: "He that diggeth a pit shall fall into it; and whoso breaketh an hedge, a serpent shall bite him" (Ecclesiastes 10:8).

God allows what we allow (See Ephesians 3:20; Matthew 9:29). Now, when God saw Job opening a door to Satan by his lack of faith that God could keep him, his family, and his possessions safe, do we really believe that God would tell Satan? No, of course not. But Satan, the accuser of the brethren (See Revelation 12:10), loves to enforce the dominion in the earth that he stole from man. He loves to demand merciless justice imposed on man when man partook of the tree of the knowledge of good and evil.

Satan knew Job had opened a door to him. And Satan knew he had the right to take advantage of that open door. Also, he knew God was legally obligated to let him. This explains why God asked, "Have you considered my servant Job?" In other words, God is saying, "Are you setting your sights on my servant Job?"

Satan hates God's servants. Do not take it personally. Satan's greatest pleasure is to destroy what God loves, and God loves us, His children. The reason Satan attacks us so vigorously is to steal God's Word in us. True knowledge, understanding, and wisdom of God's Word in us has the ability to keep Satan at bay, destroy his works, and show God's glory here on earth. This explains why Satan works so hard to keep Christians in darkness and in defeat through lack of knowledge of Who God is.

When studying Job, we need to understand how much Job is like believers today that misunderstand God. Like Job, many believers still believe that "the Lord takes as well as gives." They fail to renew their minds to the Biblical truth that God is a giver of every good and perfect gift, and His gifts are without repentance (See James 1:17; Romans 11:29).

Job is an excellent example of how Christians today misinterpret, misunderstand, or just do not know God very well. Then in our ignorance, selfishness, or self-righteousness, we stand before God trying to explain, reason, justify, or negotiate our way out of problems.

Instead, we need to study the Word of God and find the promised answer to our problem, situation, or circumstance. Then we need to stand before God boldly because we know who we are in Christ and that all of God's promises are yes and amen (See 2 Corinthians 1:20). When we truly submit to God and resist the devil, we will see Satan flee.

Even Job finally figured out that he was wrong. He stopped blaming God and recognized that God was not the problem but the solution. Through revelation knowledge by the words God spoke to Job in chapters 38 through 41, Job saw the error of his self-righteousness and self-defense, and he repented.

> THEN JOB said to the Lord,
> I know that You can do all things, and that no thought
> *or* purpose of Yours can be restrained *or* thwarted.

[You said to me] Who is this that darkens *and*
obscures counsel [by words] without knowledge? Therefore [I now see] I have [rashly]
uttered what I did not understand, things too
wonderful for me, which I did not know.
[I had virtually said to You what You have said
to me:] Hear, I beseech You, and I will speak; I
will demand of You, and You declare to me.
I had heard of You [only] by the hearing of the
ear, but now my [spiritual] eye sees You.
Therefore I loathe [my words] *and* abhor myself
and repent in dust and ashes.
(Job 42:1-6 Amp)

Once Job repented (turned from his wrong
thinking and speaking), and forgave and prayed
for his friends, God was able to move on his
behalf. "And the Lord turned the captivity of Job
and restored his fortunes, when he prayed for his
friends; also the Lord gave Job twice as much as he
had before" (Job 42:10 Amp).

Again, what I believe is the most important aspect
of Job for believers today can be summed up in this
verse: "I had heard of You [only] by the hearing of the
ear, but now my [spiritual] eye sees You" (Job 42:5 Amp).
God's personal, specific revelation to Job caused Job's
thinking, speaking, and behavior to change. With the
proper knowledge of God and the proper corresponding
action, Job was delivered from the devourer.

If Christians would understand this about Job instead of using Job as a banner for their defeated lives, God would be able to work mightily through them. Many people would see believers' lives changed and want what they have. They would want to know God personally so that their lives would change.

The study of God's Word must be more than an intellectual pursuit. The Holy Spirit must be allowed to reveal the truth of Who God is. Only then can we personally and intimately know Him. As a result, we will speak like Job, "now my spiritual eye sees You."

Faith's Opposite–Fear

Because of living in a performance-based society, many Christians have difficulty renewing their minds to the fact that Jesus Christ did everything necessary for us to live free from fear. By faith we are to rest in Him and believe that He loves us and has His very best for us. If we are still struggling to accomplish or overcome things by our own power in an effort to control life's circumstances, we are allowing fear to reign in our lives.

Fear is sometimes referred to as "False Evidence Appearing Real." Fear is having more faith in what the physical world and Satan are showing us rather than having faith in what God has said about any and all situations. Jesus said, "...In the world ye shall have tribulation: but be of good cheer; I have overcome the world" (John 16:33). In other words, don't let what you see make you afraid because I have done everything for you to be victorious. Just put your trust in Me.

If we are *not* walking in faith that operates through love, then we are walking in fear (See Galatians 5:6; 1 John 4:18). Fear is the direct opposite and opposing force of faith working by love. We must let the knowledge of God's love for us continually transform us from glory to glory. When we allow God to transform us by His Word and His Spirit, then our faith in Him will not become diluted with doubt. Fear will not be able to reign in our lives. Adam and Eve are a perfect example of the difference between living in faith or in fear.

Examine Adam and Eve's relationship with God before they sinned against Him. They had an intimate relationship with God and fellowshipped with Him daily. They were so God-conscious that they did not even consider the nakedness of their own bodies. Their attitude was much like Jesus described when explaining how Christians are to be.

> Therefore I say unto you, Take no thought for your life, what ye shall eat, or what ye shall drink; nor yet for your body, what ye shall put on. Is not the life more than meat, and the body than raiment? Behold the fowls of the air: for they sow not, neither do they reap, nor gather into barns; yet your heavenly Father feedeth them. Are ye not much better than they?
> (Matthew 6:25-26)

Adam and Eve were not worried about their next meal or how to clothe themselves. They were completely free from fear because of their perfect relationship and fellowship with God. They trusted God, Who is love, to be their provider. They had no doubt that God loved them, and their faith in God was perfect (complete).

Once they ate of the tree of knowledge of good and evil, however, their thinking, speaking, and behavior changed dramatically. In fear, they judged themselves unworthy to be in God's presence and hid from Him. They believed that God would reject them because they saw how inadequate they were in and of themselves. They became self-centered and sin-conscious and that made them cowards. Being self-centered and sin-conscious makes cowards of us all.

Jacob's Changed Identity

Jacob is a good example of how self-centeredness and sin-consciousness makes one a coward. In Genesis 32, Jacob was on his way back to the land of Canaan after 20 years. Twenty years earlier, he had fled for his life after deceitfully taking his brother Esau's birthright and blessing. Jacob had truly lived up to the meaning of his name: "heel-catcher, supplanter, cheater, defrauder, and deceiver."[1]

By the time Jacob was commanded by God to return to Canaan, God had blessed him with a large family and great material wealth. More importantly,

Jacob had God's personal guarantee that the Abrahamic covenant would continue through his line. Therefore, Jacob should have been fully persuaded that God would protect him from Esau upon his return to Canaan. But Jacob was struggling with a wrong identity. He was letting his consciousness of past sins override what God said about him. He still saw himself as he once was and *not* as the inheritor of all the promises that God had made to Abraham and then to Isaac.

As stated early, self-centeredness and sin-consciousness makes cowards of us all, and we can see this is true for Jacob as well.

> Then Jacob was greatly afraid and distressed:
> and he divided the people that *was* with him,
> and the flocks, and herds, and the camels, into
> two bands;
> And said, If Esau come to the one company, and
> smite it, then the other company which is left
> shall escape.
> **And Jacob said, O God of my father Abraham,**
> **and God of my Father Isaac, the LORD which**
> **saidst unto me, Return unto thy country, and**
> **to thy kindred, and I will deal well with thee:**
> **I am not worthy of the least of all the mer-**
> **cies, and of all the truth, which thou has**
> **showed unto thy servant**; for with my staff I
> passed over this Jordan; and now I am be-
> come two bands.

> **Deliver me, I pray thee, from the hand of my**
> **brother, from the hand of Esau: for I fear him,**
> lest he will come and smite me, *and* the mother
> with the children.
> **And thou saidst, I will surely do thee good**
> **and make thy seed as the sand of the sea,**
> **which cannot be numbered for multitude.**
> (Genesis 32:7-12, *emphasis mine*)

God had told Jacob he would be with him, yet Jacob was afraid. But rather than run from God, Jacob does what God wants all His children to do. Jacob got alone with God, the Lord, the Word and wrestled until he received a blessing from God, the Lord, the Word.

How many of us today wrestle with the Word until we receive revelation by the Spirit of God that brings the blessing? God promises that if we draw near to him, he will draw near to us.

> Submit yourselves therefore to God. Resist the
> devil, and he will flee from you.
> **Draw nigh to God, and he will draw nigh to**
> **you.** Cleanse *your* hands, *ye* sinners; and purify
> *your* hearts, *ye* double minded.
> Be afflicted, and mourn, and weep: let your laughter
> be turned to mourning, and *your* joy to heaviness.
> Humble yourselves in the sight of the Lord, and
> he shall lift you up.
> (James 4:7-10, *emphasis mine*)

Jacob's fear was a clear indication that he was not yet fully persuaded. He was double-minded about God's promised protection and blessing, but he made a decision to wrestle with God's spoken promises in prayer. "Yea, he had power over the angel, and prevailed: he wept, and made supplication unto him…" (Hosea 12:4).

The previous Scripture is about what Jacob did to prevail, and we are to do the same. When a promise of God is hard for us to believe by faith and fear grips us, we need to get alone with God, wrestle with the Word until we prevail in prayer.

> Be careful for nothing; but in every thing by prayer and supplication with thanksgiving let your requests be made known unto God.
> And the peace of God, which passeth all understanding, shall keep your hearts and minds through Christ Jesus.
> (Philippians 4:6-7)

Christians have to stop "religiousizing" (making of none effect) the Word of God. We need to recognize God's Word as Jesus Christ, the spoken Word of God made flesh. When properly understood and applied, God's Word will cause a change in this physical world. If we are struggling to believe His Word, it is our responsibility to wrestle in prayer and prevail over all the doubt and unbelief that causes fear. Fear kills faith. But

through prayer, a two-way conversation with God, we
will become fully persuaded about His blessing.

The Blessing of Abraham

What is the blessing of Abraham? The blessing is
grace–the good will, loving-kindness, and favor of God.[2]

> NOW [IN Haran] the Lord said to Abram,
> Go for yourself [for your own advantage]
> away from your country, from your relatives
> and your father's house, to the land that I
> will show you.
> And I will make of you a great nation, and **I
> will bless you [with abundant increase of
> favors]** and make your name famous *and* dis-
> tinguished, and you will be a blessing [dispens-
> ing good to others].
> And I will bless those who bless you [who
> confer prosperity or happiness upon you] and
> curse him who curses *or* uses insolent language
> toward you; in you will all the families *and* kin-
> dred of the earth be blessed [and by you they
> will bless, themselves].
> So Abram departed, as the Lord had directed him;…
> (Genesis 12:1-4 Amp, *emphasis mine*)

What was required of Abraham to receive the
blessing? Abraham had to believe and have faith in

God. And because he believed, God declared Abraham righteous–innocent, faultless, and guiltless.[3]

> **Thus Abraham believed in *and* adhered to *and* trusted in and relied on God, and it was reckoned *and* placed to his account *and* credited as righteousness (as conformity to the divine will in purpose, thought, and action).** Know *and* understand that it is [really] the people [who live] by faith who are [the true] sons of Abraham.
>
> And the Scripture, foreseeing that God would justify (declare righteous, put in right standing with Himself) the Gentiles in consequence of faith, **proclaimed the Gospel [foretelling the glad tidings of a Savior long beforehand] to Abraham in the promise, saying, In you shall all the nations [of the earth] be blessed.** So then, those who are people of faith are blessed and made happy *and* favored by God [as partners in fellowship] with the believing *and* trusting Abraham.
>
> (Galatians 3:6-9 Amp, *emphasis mine*)

Righteousness by faith (right standing with God through faith in Him) caused Abraham to receive the blessing of God. But Galatians 3:8 reveals more specifically what Abraham believed. Abraham's belief rested in the promise of a future Savior, Jesus Christ.

Jesus testified to this when He said that Abraham saw His day (See John 8:56). As alluded to in the fourth chapter of this book, Scripture indicates that Isaac also saw Jesus' day, and through righteousness by faith received the blessing of Abraham. And Jacob received the blessing through righteousness by faith, too.

Before Jacob was sent away to his uncle, Laban, his father, Isaac, prophesied that Jacob would receive the blessing of Abraham.

> And God Almighty bless thee, and make thee fruitful, and multiply thee, that thou mayest be a multitude of people;
> **And give thee the blessing of Abraham**, to thee, and to thy seed with thee; that thou mayest inherit the land wherein thou art a stranger, which God gave unto Abraham.
> (Genesis 28:3-4, *emphasis mine*)

I believe that Jacob knew exactly what the blessing was. He knew the blessing of God was the unmerited favor received through righteousness by faith–100% acceptance by God based on the belief in a future Messiah, Jesus Christ.

Jacob had grown up hearing the stories of Abraham and Isaac's encounters with God. He had heard about God's provision of a substitutionary sacrifice killed in Isaac's place. Again, Jesus himself said that Abraham saw His day (See John 8:56). He had heard all his life about

God, but, just like Job, hearing with physical ears is not enough. One needs to see the blessing with spiritual eyes and then receive it by faith. So, Jacob became determined in his heart not to let go of God, the Lord, the Word, until he received the blessing of Abraham–God's unmerited favor through righteousness by faith.

How do we know that Jacob received the blessing of Abraham? We know because the Bible tells us he was blessed after wrestling all night with the angel of the Lord. But before the blessing of Abraham came, Jacob's identity was changed. Instead of Jacob, the deceiver, he was renamed Israel, a prince that has power with God and with men and prevailed (See Genesis 32:28).

Jacob's self-centeredness and sin-consciousness were put to death. Because of his new identity, he was able to see God and receive eternal life. "…For I have seen God face to face, and my life is preserved" (Genesis 32:30).

Still another way in which we see the blessing of Abraham come upon Jacob is that his walk was forever changed. By becoming righteous by faith, Jacob's walk in the world was different. Jacob was wounded yet healed. God removed his old identity and made him into a new man. But he bore the marks in his body of his victory in receiving the blessing of Abraham. This mark was his changed walk.

This supernatural wounding and healing can be seen in Jesus' life. First, Jesus was wounded and crucified to fulfill the specific plans and purposes of God. But three days later Jesus was raised from the dead in victory by conquering sin and death and bringing redemption to man through belief in Him. He continues to this day, however, to bare the marks in His body of that victory.

As Christians, we must allow the Word, the two-edged sword, to do its work (See 2 Timothy 2:15-17). We must allow the Word to wound our hearts by cutting out those things not of God, yet we must allow the Word to heal our hearts so that we can love God's way. And, yes, we will bare the same marks in our body as the body of Christ. "Dying to self" will have the marks of crucified flesh, and our walk will be forever changed. We will no longer walk according to the flesh, but we will walk according to the Spirit of God.

Through His Word, our loving heavenly Father trains, corrects, and disciplines.

> **For the Lord corrects *and* disciplines everyone whom He loves,** and He punishes, even scourges, every son whom He accepts *and* welcomes to His heart *and* cherishes.
> You must submit to *and* endure [correction] for discipline; God is dealing with you as with sons. For what son is there whom his father does not [thus] train *and* correct and discipline? Now if you are exempt from correction *and* left without discipline in which all [of God's children] share, then you are illegitimate offspring *and* not true sons [at all].

Moreover, we have had earthly fathers who disciplined us and we yielded [to them] *and* respected [them for training us]. Shall we not much more cheerfully submit to the Father of spirits and so [truly] live?

For [our earthly fathers] disciplined us for only a short period of time *and* chastised us as seemed proper *and* good to them; but **He disciplines us for our certain good, that we may become sharers in His own holiness.**

For the time being no discipline brings joy, but seems grievous *and* painful; **but afterwards it yields a peaceable fruit of righteousness** to those who have been trained by it **[a harvest of fruit which consists in righteousness—in conformity to God's will in purpose, thought, and action, resulting in right living and right standing with God].**

(Hebrews 12:6-11 Amp, *emphasis mine*)

Jacob received the new spirit of Israel, his new identity, to fulfill the plan and purpose of God for his life. He went out after that to face his persecutor, Esau, and was totally victorious in the end.

We are to do the same. We are to embrace our new identity in Christ, and, by faith in Jesus Christ, we are to fulfill the plan and purpose of God for our lives. Once we are fully persuaded that all things are possible through Christ Jesus, we will face our persecutors with total confidence that we have the victory in Jesus Christ's finished work. We will have no fear because we know God (love), and perfect love has cast out all fear. We will walk in the blessing of Abraham (See Galatians 3:13-14).

Grace

Before I came to Christ, I believed God was mean and was angry with me because of His disgust for me. Not until God sent three people to me, who knew the true nature of God, was I convinced that God loved a sinner like me.

When I received Jesus as my Lord and Savior, I had no idea what I had. In my limited knowledge, *grace* was what families recited over their evening meals. My husband, Bob, was the first to tell me about grace in a way that I could understand. He told me I could not earn God's grace. God's unearned or unmerited love, favor and ability could only be received through believing and trusting in Jesus Christ. He told me that through Jesus, grace was a free gift from God. Here I was a born again, child of God, but I just could not believe that anything was free.

Bob continued by explaining that I was 100% accepted by God the day I received Jesus into my heart. He said to imagine God wearing "Jesus sunglasses." He explained that when God looks at us, He sees only Jesus. Through grace God loves us unconditionally because of who we are in Christ and not because of our performance.

I remember so clearly how strange that sounded because I had lived in a world for forty years where love and acceptance was based on my performance. Completely confused, I asked the question, "Well, if God doesn't care about my performance, what keeps me from sinning all I want?"

He answered, "You will *not* want to sin. As you become more personally and intimately involved with God, you will be amazed at how He will change your heart—your desires. You will do things for God *not* because you *have to* but because you *want to*. As God begins to show you how much He loves you, you will fall in love with Him. You will *not* serve Him out of fear that He will hurt or reject you, but you will serve Him out of love." Then Bob showed me various Scriptures that supported his explanation. From all those he showed me, the following Scripture had the most dramatic impact.

> But God commendeth his love toward us, in that,
> while we were yet sinners, Christ died for us.
> **Much more then,** being now justified by his
> blood, we shall be saved from wrath through him.
> For if, when we were enemies, we were recon-
> ciled to God by the death of his Son, **much more,**
> being reconciled, we shall be saved by his life.
> And not only *so,* but **we also joy in God**
> through our Lord Jesus Christ, by whom we
> have now received the atonement.
> (Romans 5:8-11, *emphasis mine*)

I saw that God had always loved me, even when I had not loved Him. I had not become suddenly good enough for Him to accept me, but I had realized finally that God was the only one who could save me from the disastrous life I was living. He received me just as I was. And now that I was His child, I saw that He loved me even more. He had not revealed to me His unconditional love when I was a sinner just to turn His wrath upon me now that I was His child. I saw that I was to enjoy and to love Him just as much as He enjoyed and loved me.

I became convinced that my image of God and myself had to change if I was to successfully live out my new identity in Christ. Just as Job and Jacob, I had to have spiritual eyes to see. I had to wrestle with the Word of God to obtain the blessing of it by the revelation of the Holy Spirit.

Confusion Does Not Come from God

Scripture tells us that God is not the author of confusion (See 1 Corinthians 14:33). Then why is there so much confusion about God's true nature and character even for Christians that study His Word. Personally, I believe the confusion comes from not understanding the difference between God's dealings with people under the Law of Moses and His dealings with people under the New Testament. Today's believers are trying to live under both the law of works and the law of faith through grace. As a result, they are becoming confused, deceived, and defeated. Jesus tells us, God never intended us to live under both.

> He told them this parable: "No one tears a
> patch from a new garment and sews it on an
> old one. If he does, he will have torn the new
> garment, and the patch from the new will not
> match the old.
> And no one pours new wine into old wineskins.
> If he does, the new wine will burst the skins, the
> wine will run out and the wineskins will be ruined.
> No, new wine must be poured into new wineskins.
> And no one after drinking old wine wants the
> new. For he says, 'the old is better.'"
> (Luke 5:36-39 NIV)

Paul's ministry was spent preaching the "good news" of the New Testament. We have been freed from the law of works through Jesus Christ.

> Tell me, you who are bent on being under
> the Law, will you listen to what the Law
> [really] says?
> For it is written that Abraham had two sons, one
> by the bondmaid and one by the free woman.
> But whereas the child of the slave woman was
> born according to the flesh *and* had an ordinary
> birth, the son of the free woman was born in
> fulfillment of the promise.

Now all this is an allegory; these [two wom-
en] represent two covenants. One covenant
originated from Mount Sinai [where the Law
was given] and bears [children destined] for
slavery; this is Hagar.

Now Hagar is (stands for) Mount Sinai in Ara-
bia and she corresponds to *and* belongs in the
same category with the present Jerusalem, for
she is in bondage together with her children.
But the Jerusalem above (the Messianic Kingdom of Christ) is free, and she is our mother.
For it is written in the Scriptures, Rejoice, O
barren woman, who has not given birth to
children; break forth into a joyful shout, you
who are not feeling birth pangs, for the desolate woman has many more children than she
who has a husband.

But we, brethren, are children [not by physical
descent, as was Ishmael, but] like Isaac, born in
virtue of promise.

Yet [just] as at that time the child [of ordinary
birth] born according to the flesh despised *and*
persecuted him [who was born remarkably] according to [the promise and the working of] the
[Holy] Spirit, so it is now also.

But what does the Scripture say? Cast out *and* send
away the slave woman and her son, for never shall
the son of the slave woman be heir *and* share in
inheritance with the son of the free woman.

So, brethren, [we who are born again] are not
children of a slave woman [the natural], but of
the free [the supernatural].
IN [THIS] freedom Christ has made us free
[and completely liberated us]; stand fast then,
and do not be hampered *and* held ensnared *and*
submit again to a yoke of slavery [which you
have once put off].
(Galatians 4:21-31 and 5:1 Amp)

Praise God! This is the "too good to be true" news
of the gospel of Jesus Christ that I once had trouble
understanding. Once I began to study God's Word
through the power of the Holy Spirit, however, I saw
myself changed just as my husband told me. My new
identity is in Jesus Christ as a member of His body. My
heavenly Father loves me no matter what I do. The things
I do for Him I do because I love Him. His desires are my
desires because He is changing me daily into His son's
image. I am living that transformed life that the gift of
God's grace has made possible. I come boldly to the
throne of grace, and there I am strengthened, not beaten
like a dog. I am fully persuaded that God loves me.

THEREFORE BEING justified by faith, we have
peace with God through our Lord Jesus Christ:
By whom also we have access by faith into this
grace wherein we stand, and rejoice in hope of
the glory of God.

And not only *so*, but we glory in tribulations
also: knowing that tribulation worketh patience;
And patience, experience; and experience, hope:
And hope maketh not ashamed; because the
love of God is shed abroad in our hearts by the
Holy Ghost which is given unto us.
(Romans 5:1-5)

Righteousness by Faith Supersedes the Law of Works

1. *The Holy Spirit is only received by faith:*[4] Paul
admonished the Galatians not to mix faith and works. He
tells them the Holy Spirit can only be received by faith
in Jesus, not in the works of the flesh. He goes on to tell
them that faith in Jesus can only come by hearing the
Word of faith. The Galatians were trying to do by works
what can only be done through God's Spirit.

O FOOLISH Galatians, who hath bewitched
you, that ye should not obey the truth, before
whose eyes Jesus Christ hath been evidently
set forth, crucified among you?
This only would I learn of you, Received ye
the Spirit by the works of the law, or by the
hearing of faith?
Are ye so foolish? having begun in the Spirit,
are ye now made perfect by the flesh?
Have ye suffered so many things in vain? if *it*
be yet in vain.

He therefore that ministereth to you the Spirit,
and worketh miracles among you, *doeth he it* by
the works of the law, or by the hearing of faith?
(Galatians 3:1-5)

2. *The Gifts of the Spirit are worked by faith not by the law of works:*[5] Paul further explains that God preached the "good news" of salvation to Abraham, and because Abraham believed, God called him righteous. Those that accept Jesus as their Savior receive the blessing of Abraham, God's unmerited favor through right standing with Him.

Even as Abraham believed God, and it was accounted to him for righteousness.
Know ye therefore that they which are of faith,
the same are the children of Abraham.
And the scripture, foreseeing that God would
justify the heathen through faith, preached
before the gospel unto Abraham, *saying*, In thee
shall all nations be blessed.
So then they which be of faith are blessed with
faithful Abraham.
(Galatians 3:6-9)

3. *All under the law are under the curse:*[6] Paul wanted the Galatians to understand that those that continue to refuse Jesus and rely on their own works for salvation live accursed. A man's works (self-righteousness) can never justify his sin nature before a holy God. God's holy

standards set down in the law were never intended to justify man and appease the wrath of God. Only faith in Jesus, as our complete and perfect sacrifice and payment for sin, could do this.

> For as many as are of the works of the law are under the curse: for it is written, Cursed *is* every one that continueth not in all things which are written in the book of the law to do them. But that no man is justified by the law in the sight of God, *it is* evident: for, **The just shall live by faith. And the law is not of faith:** but, The man that doeth them shall live in them.
> (Galatians 3:10-12, *emphasis mine*)

4. *Christ bore the curse of the law to bring us the blessing:*[7] Paul explains that those who will trust in and rely on Jesus will be delivered from the curse of the law through justification by faith and thereby receive the promise of the Holy Spirit. Then the Holy Spirit will lead and guide us into all truth.

> Christ hath redeemed us from the curse of the law, being made a curse for us: for it is written, Cursed *is* every one that hangeth on a tree: That the blessing of Abraham might come on the Gentiles through Jesus Christ; that we might receive the promise of the Spirit through faith.
> (Galatians 3:13-14)

5. *God's inheritance comes by the Abrahamic faith-covenant not the law of works:* Paul tells them again that the law was never designed to replace or add to the faith-covenant God made with Abraham. Paul makes it very clear that the seed of Abraham is Jesus Christ. Through the acceptance of Jesus, we become the body of Christ and thereby become the seed of Abraham to whom God's inheritance is promised.

> Brethren, I speak after the manner of men;
> Though *it be* but a man's covenant, yet *if it be* confirmed, no man disannulleth, or addeth thereto.
> Now to Abraham and his seed were the promises made. He saith not, And to seeds, as of many; but as of one, And to thy seed, which is Christ.
> And this I say, *that* the covenant, that was confirmed before of God in Christ, the law, which was four hundred and thirty years after, cannot disannul, that it should make the promise of none effect.
> For if the inheritance *be* of the law, *it is* no more of promise: but God gave *it* to Abraham by promise. (Galatians 3:15-18)

6. *The real reason for the law:*[8] Paul clearly states that the law was given because of transgressions or sin. Before the law, God was extending His grace toward man. "For until the law sin was in the world: but sin is not imputed when there is no law" (Romans 5:13).

"Sin is not imputed" means that people's sins were not counted against them. But by reading the accounts of man before the law, it becomes clear that man did not understand what God was doing. Instead of man coming to repentance because God withheld His wrath and extended His love, grace and mercy, they saw it as permission to sin.

An account from Genesis 4 explains how easily man had misinterpreted God's attitude toward sin. Cain's great-great-great grandson, Lemech, was the first polygamist and the second murderer mentioned in the Bible. Lemech told his wives that he had killed a young man that had wounded him. Therefore, Lemech reasoned that if God would avenge Cain sevenfold for a premeditated murder, then God would avenge him seventy-sevenfold for murdering a man in self-defense.

We can see from this example that man did not have an accurate understanding of God and God's abhorrence of sin. Through lack of knowledge, man was being destroyed by sin. Eventually, God had to rid the earth of such corruption before no one was left to bring forth the seed of Abraham, Jesus. The saving of Noah and his family to preserve the seed was an act of divine love, grace, and mercy. God knew that Jesus, our mediator, was the only one who could bring salvation to the world.

> Wherefore then *serveth* the law? It was
> added because of transgressions, till the
> seed should come to whom the promise was

made; *and it* was ordained by angels in the
hand of a mediator.
Now a mediator is not *a mediator* of one, but
God is one.
(Galatians 3:19-20)

7. *The law was of God to show man how far they had
fallen:* The law of works cannot save but can only bring
man into an awareness of sin and death. When the law
came, so did the acute awareness of temptation, sin,
and death. The sin nature in man becomes even more
rebellious.

I heard a pastor tell of an experiment he performed
to demonstrate the effects of the law. His son and some
friends had been playing for sometime in the yard
completely unaware of a lone flower close to the house.
Eventually, the pastor went outside and gathered the
boys around the flower. In an authoritative voice, he
instructed them not to spit on that flower. Then he sent
them off to play again.

The pastor went inside and watched the boys.
Within minutes, he saw nearly half of the boys spit on
that flower while the others stood and watched. A flower
that had been totally unnoticed by the boys earlier had
become a temptation once a restriction or a law was put
in place.

God's law to the Israelites was completely holy and
just. And it accomplished exactly what God intended
it to do. He had designed the law to be a schoolmaster.

The law was to show man that they could not possibly become as holy as God through their own self-effort and self-righteousness. No, the law showed a need for a savior that became our righteousness. Jesus Christ's work brought us back into right relationship and fellowship with God, our Father.

> *Is* the law then against the promises of God?
> God forbid: for if there had been a law given
> which could have given life, verily righteous-
> ness should have been by the law.
> But the scripture hath concluded all under sin,
> that the promise by faith of Jesus Christ might
> be given to them that believe.
> But before faith came, we were kept under the
> law, shut up unto the faith, which should after-
> wards be revealed.
> **Wherefore the law was our schoolmaster**
> *to bring us* **unto Christ, that we might be**
> **justified by faith.**
> (Galatians 3:21-24, *emphasis mine*)

8. *Faith in Jesus liberates us from the law of works:*[9] In Paul's next statement, he has made it very clear that we no longer live under the schoolmaster (the law of works), but we live by faith in Jesus alone. Our belief that we are 100% loved and accepted by God because of our faith in Jesus enables us to come boldly before God (See Hebrews 4:16). Not boldness out of arrogance, but

boldness through knowledge of who we are in Christ. I know that I can ask anything according to God's Word (Jesus), and He hears me. And if he hears me, I know that He will grant my request (See 1 John 5:14-15). He does this because He said He would. God does not lie.

Over the years, I have become fully persuaded that God not only loves me, but He actually likes me. This revelation can only come by spending time with Him. Through prayer and study, I have an ever-increasing intimacy with God that helps to keep Him ever present in my daily life.

God has told us in Hosea that His people are destroyed for lack of knowledge. The knowledge they lack is the knowledge of a personal loving relationship and fellowship with our living God.

> But after that faith is come, we are no longer
> under a schoolmaster.
> (Galatians 3:25)

9. *Faith in Jesus makes us heirs as sons and daughters in God's family:*[10] Once we become righteous through Jesus Christ, we do not need the law and the bondage that it placed in us. We are free to live by faith in Him and in the new identity he has given us. We are dead to our sin nature, and we are alive unto Christ.

Christ gave His life for us, to give His life to us, to live His life through us. We are not allowing Christ to live His life through us if we are still bound to the do's and

don'ts of the law. We no longer live our lives according
to the flesh, but we live our lives as part of the body of
Christ. We submit ourselves to His Spirit dwelling in
us. By faith, not the law, we live our lives as sons and
daughters of our heavenly Father.

> For ye are all the children of God by faith in
> Christ Jesus.
> For as many of you as have been baptized into
> Christ have put on Christ.
> There is neither Jew nor Greek, there is neither
> bond nor free, there is neither male nor female:
> for ye are all one in Christ Jesus.
> And if ye *be* Christ's, then are ye Abraham's
> seed, and heirs according to the promise.
> (Galatians 3:26-29)

10. *The goodness of God leads us to turn from evil:*
Once we see that we cannot justify ourselves and obtain
right standing with God through self-righteousness by
keeping the law, then we are able to see how merciful
and gracious God is to withhold His wrath and give us
grace through Jesus. By sacrificing Jesus in our place,
we can see the goodness of God. And according to
Scripture, the goodness of God, not the law of God,
leads us to repentance.

> But we are sure that the judgment of God is accord-
> ing to truth against them, which commit such things.

And thinkest thou this, O man, that judgest
them which do such things, and doest the same,
that thou shalt escape the judgment of God?
Or despisest thou the riches of his goodness and forbearance and longsuffering; not
knowing that **the goodness of God leadeth
thee to repentance?**
(Romans 2:2-4, *emphasis mine*)

Once again "God is not the author of confusion."
Jesus is the author of our faith (See Hebrews 12:2). Satan
is the author of confusion. He has caused Christians
to stumble in the darkness of unbelief. He has caused
Christians to believe that they must continue to live
under the covenant of the law of works.

Remember daily, Jesus has come to give us
abundant life. If something tries to steal, kill, or destroy
that life (See John 10:10), we are commanded to resist it
(See James 4:7). Resist it with the absolute truth of God's
Word and by the power of God's Spirit. We are the army
of Christ. And as His army, we are to battle from the
position of Christ's victory.

Lessons from the Israelites:
The Veil of Moses Unveiled through Christ

Moses was the lawgiver according to Scripture. He was the one who received from God His perfect requirement for holiness. And what did this perfect letter of the law written on tablets of stone produce? The law produced hearts of stone in those who arrogantly thought they could fulfill the law in their own self-effort.

Throughout Exodus God refers to His people as stiff-necked people. Yet, Moses, a friend of God, had a different spirit. This different spirit is evident in Exodus 34 after Moses returned with the second set of stone tablets. He had spent forty days in the presence of God, and when the Israelites saw him, they were afraid. Moses' face was aglow with the glory of God and that made the Israelites draw back in the same way they did earlier when God's glory was manifested on the mount (See Exodus 20). Once again their evil hearts of unbelief kept them from enjoying God's intimacy and grace.

God's glory showed so bright in Moses' face that he veiled his face in the midst of these stiffed-necked people. The veil is a type and shadow of those who demand the letter of the law but will always be blinded from the glory God wants to display in our hearts through the life of Jesus Christ.

But notice the heart of Moses that comes from a intimate relationship with God. Moses took the veil off in the presence of the Lord. In God's glorious presence, no separation from God exists. Only joy exists in meeting with God face-to-face like a friend. Moses' and the Israelites' relationship with God was different when one observes the times that the veil was on or off as Moses went in and out of God's presence (See Exodus 34).

The veil of Moses can be compared to the veils (varying degrees of separation) that were constructed for the temple. The veil that separated the Israelites from God's presence in the Holy of Holies is the most significant. God rent that veil at Calvary to show His total forgiveness and acceptance of us through our faith in Jesus Christ.

Scripture has revealed how the veiled hearts of the Israelites kept them blinded to the love and acceptance of God. We are much the same if we choose to continue in the law (works) rather than the full liberty of faith in Jesus Christ (grace).

> But their minds were blinded: for until this day remaineth the same veil untaken away in the reading of the old testament; which *veil* is done away in Christ.
> But even unto this day, when Moses is read, the veil is upon their hearts.
> Nevertheless when it shall turn to the Lord, the veil shall be taken away.

Now the Lord is that Spirit: and where the
Spirit of the Lord *is*, there *is* liberty.
But we all, with open face beholding as in a
glass the glory of the Lord, are changed into the
same image from glory to glory, *even* as by the
Spirit of the Lord.
(2 Corinthians 3:14-18)

What we can see through the example of the
Israelites is that with God everything is about one's heart.
The law was never designed to make us love God with
all of our hearts and minds. The law was never designed
to show us the total picture of God's love.

The law was designed to show us our pride in the
midst of His perfect moral government. The law was
designed to break us of thinking we could approach God
in our own self-righteousness. The law was designed
to bring us to the conclusion that we needed a perfect
savior–One that brings us into right standing with God.

Scripture is clear that our perfect savior is
Jesus Christ.

Then said he, Lo, I come to do thy will, O
God. He taketh away the first, that he may
establish the second....
This *is* the covenant that I will make with
them after those days, saith the Lord, I will
put my laws into their hearts, and in their
minds will I write them;

And their sins and iniquities will I remember
no more.
Now where remission of these is, *there is* no
more offering for sin.
Having therefore, brethren, boldness to en-
ter into the holiest by the blood of Jesus,
By a new and living way, which he hath
consecrated for us, through the veil, that is
to say, his flesh;
And *having* an high priest over the house of God;
Let us draw near with a true heart in full assurance of faith, having our hearts sprinkled
from an evil conscience, and our bodies
washed with pure water.
Let us hold fast the profession of *our* faith without wavering; (for he *is* faithful that promised;).
(Hebrews 10:9, and 16-23, *emphasis mine*)

Please see that the law veiled God's true nature by
showing us only God's moral mandates for holiness. But
through Jesus Christ, we are now invited to come boldly to
the true, living God of grace. Don't let the veil of legalism
ensnare and blind. Let faith in Christ Jesus unveil the truth
of Who God is. God is love, and He "so loved the world
He sent His only begotten Son" to redeem us.

When the disciples asked Jesus to teach them to
pray, Jesus had not finished His work. Therefore, He told
them to pray that God not lead them into temptation
but to deliver them from evil. This Scripture bothered

me in light of the passage in James that assures us that God does not tempt us with evil. What I have come to understand is that Jesus was telling His disciples to ask God to no longer lead them by the law that causes sin to come alive, but to bring the Savior Who would deliver them from all evil.

I saw that Jesus was encouraging them to expect God to do away with the law of sin and death (the curse of the law) because the Savior would conquer sin and death. This assures me that in the finished work of Jesus Christ alone, we are blessed. We can take none of the credit for the blessing because Jesus deserves all the glory for it.

The Israelites could only be blessed by their own obedience to the do's and don'ts of the law–the law of the flesh. But we live by Jesus Christ's obedience and fulfillment of the law. We are to live by grace, God's unmerited favor and ability. We are to live by faith in the finished work of Christ Jesus and the work of the Holy Spirit. We are to live by "faith that works by love" not by "faith in self-effort."

When the veil of doubt and confusion is removed, we can know Him and the One He sent. According to John 17:3, this is eternal life, but few Christians seem to know this.

In concluding this examination of God's true nature and character, I again encourage you to make this request, "Will the real God please stand up?" Then trust that God will reveal Himself. "But without faith *it is* impossible to please *him*: for he that cometh to God **must believe that he is,** and *that* **he is a rewarder of those who diligently seek him**" (Hebrews 11:6, *emphasis mine*).

Appendix A:
The Blessings and Curses of the Law

Deuteronomy 28:1-14
The Blessings of the Law

28:1   AND IT shall come to pass, if thou shalt hearken diligently unto the voice of the LORD thy God, to observe *and* to do all his commandments which I command thee this day, that the LORD thy God will set thee on high above all nations of the earth:

28:2   And all these blessings shall come on thee, and overtake thee, if thou shalt hearken unto the voice of the LORD thy God.

28:3   Blessed *shalt* thou *be* in the city, and blessed *shalt* thou *be* in the field.

28:4   Blessed *shall be* the fruit of thy body, and the fruit of thy ground, and the fruit of thy cattle, the increase of thy kine, and the flocks of thy sheep.

28:5   Blessed *shall be* thy basket and thy store.

28:6   Blessed *shalt* thou *be* when thou comest in, and blessed *shalt* thou *be* when thou goest out.

28:7   The LORD shall cause thine enemies that rise up against thee to be smitten before thy face: they shall come out against thee one way, and flee before thee seven ways.

28:8   The Lord shall command the blessing upon thee
in thy storehouses, and in all that thou settest
thine hand unto; and he shall bless thee in the land
which the Lord thy God giveth thee.

28:9   The Lord shall establish thee an holy people unto
himself, as he hath sworn unto thee, if thou shalt
keep the commandments of the Lord thy God, and
walk in his ways.

28:10   And all people of the earth shall see that thou art
called by the name of the Lord; and they shall be
afraid of thee.

28:11   And the Lord shall make thee plenteous in
goods, in the fruit of thy body, and in the fruit of
thy cattle, and in the fruit of thy ground, in the
land which the Lord sware unto thy fathers to
give thee.

28:12   The Lord shall open unto thee his good treasure,
the heaven to give the rain unto thy land in his
season, and to bless all the work of thine hand:
and thou shalt lend unto many nations, and thou
shalt not borrow.

28:13   And the Lord shall make thee the head, and not
the tail; and thou shalt be above only, and thou
shalt not be beneath; if that thou hearken unto
the commandments of the Lord thy God, which I
command thee this day, to observe and to do *them*:

28:14   And thou shalt not go aside from any of the words
which I command thee this day, *to* the right hand,
or *to* the left, to go after other gods to serve them.

Deuteronomy 28:15-68
Curses of the Law

28:15 But it shall come to pass, if thou wilt not hearken unto the voice of the LORD thy God, to observe to do all his commandments and his statutes which I command thee this day; that all these curses shall come upon thee, and overtake thee:

28:16 Cursed *shalt* thou *be* in the city, and cursed *shalt* thou *be* in the field.

28:17 Cursed *shall be* thy basket and thy store.

28:18 Cursed *shall be* the fruit of thy body, and the fruit of thy land, the increase of thy kine, and the flocks of thy sheep.

28:19 Cursed *shalt* thou *be* when thou comest in, and cursed *shalt* thou *be* when thou goest out.

28:20 The LORD shall send upon thee cursing, vexation, and rebuke, in all that thou settest thine hand unto for to do, until thou be destroyed, and until thou perish quickly; because of the wickedness of thy doings, whereby thou hast forsaken me.

28:21 The LORD shall make the pestilence cleave unto thee, until he have consumed thee from off the land, whither thou goest to possess it.

28:22 The LORD shall smite thee with a consumption, and with a fever, and with an inflammation, and with an extreme burning, and with the sword, and with blasting, and with mildew; and they shall pursue thee until thou perish.

28:23 And thy heaven that is over thy head shall be
brass, and the earth that *is* under thee *shall be* iron.

28:24 The LORD shall make the rain of thy land powder
and dust: from heaven shall it come down upon
thee, until thou be destroyed.

28:25 The LORD shall cause thee to be smitten before
thine enemies: thou shalt go out one way against
them, and flee seven ways before them: and shalt
be removed into all the kingdoms of the earth.

28:26 And thy carcase shall be meat unto all fowls of the
air, and unto the beasts of the earth, and no man
shall fray *them* away.

28:27 The LORD will smite thee with the botch of Egypt,
and with the emerods, and with the scab, and with
the itch, whereof thou canst not be healed.

28:28 The LORD shall smite thee with madness, and
blindness, and astonishment of heart:

28:29 And thou shalt grope at noonday, as the blind
gropeth in darkness, and thou shalt not prosper in
thy ways: and thou shalt be only oppressed and
spoiled evermore, and no man shall save *thee*.

28:30 Thou shalt betroth a wife, and another man
shall lie with her: thou shalt build an house, and
thou shalt not dwell therein: thou shalt plant a
vineyard, and shalt not gather the grapes thereof.

28:31 Thine ox *shall be* slain before thine eyes, and
thou shalt not eat thereof: thine ass *shall be*
violently taken away from before thy face, and
shall not be restored to thee: thy sheep *shall be*

given unto thine enemies, and thou shalt have none to rescue *them*.

28:32 Thy sons and thy daughters *shall be* given unto another people, and thine eyes shall look, and fail with longing for them all the day long: and *there shall be* no might in thine hand.

28:33 The fruit of thy land, and all thy labours, shall a nation which thou knowest not eat up; and thou shalt be only oppressed and crushed always:

28:34 So that thou shalt be mad for the sight of thine eyes which thou shalt see.

28:35 The LORD shall smite thee in the knees, and in the legs, with a sore botch that cannot be healed, from the sole of thy foot unto the top of thy head.

28:36 The LORD shall bring thee, and thy king which thou shalt set over thee, unto a nation which neither thou nor thy fathers have known; and there shalt thou serve other gods, wood and stone.

28:37 And thou shalt become an astonishment, a proverb, and a byword, among all nations whither the LORD shall lead thee.

28:38 Thou shalt carry much seed out into the field, and shalt gather *but* little in; for the locust shall consume it.

28:39 Thou shalt plant vineyards, and dress *them*, but shalt neither drink *of* the wine, nor gather *the grapes*; for the worms shall eat them.

28:40   Thou shalt have olive trees throughout all thy coasts, but thou shalt not anoint *thyself* with the oil; for thine olive shall cast *his fruit*.

28:41   Thou shalt beget sons and daughters, but thou shalt not enjoy them; for they shall go into captivity.

28:42   All thy trees and fruit of thy land shall the locust consume.

28:43   The stranger that *is* within thee shall get up above thee very high; and thou shalt come down very low.

28:44   He shall lend to thee, and thou shalt not lend to him: he shall be the head, and thou shalt be the tail.

28:45   Moreover all these curses shall come upon thee, and shall pursue thee, and overtake thee, till thou be destroyed; because thou hearkenedst not unto the voice of the LORD thy God, to keep his commandments and his statutes which he commanded thee:

28:46   And they shall be upon thee for a sign and for a wonder, and upon thy seed for ever.

28:47   Because thou servedst not the LORD thy God with joyfulness, and with gladness of heart, for the abundance of all *things*;

28:48   Therefore shalt thou serve thine enemies which the LORD shall send against thee, in hunger, and in thirst, and in nakedness, and in want of all *things*: and he shall put a yoke of iron upon thy neck, until he have destroyed thee.

28:49 The LORD shall bring a nation against thee from far, from the end of the earth, *as swift* as the eagle flieth; a nation whose tongue thou shalt not understand;

28:50 A nation of fierce countenance, which shall not regard the person of the old, nor shew favour to the young:

28:51 And he shall eat the fruit of thy cattle, and the fruit of thy land, until thou be destroyed: which *also* shall not leave thee *either* corn, wine, *or* oil, or the increase of thy kine, or flocks of thy sheep, until he have destroyed thee.

28:52 And he shall besiege thee in all thy gates, until thy high and fenced walls come down, wherein thou trustedst, throughout all thy land: and he shall besiege thee in all thy gates throughout all thy land, which the LORD thy God hath given thee.

28:53 And thou shalt eat the fruit of thine own body, the flesh of thy sons and of thy daughters, which the LORD thy God hath given thee, in the siege, and in the straitness, wherewith thine enemies shall distress thee:

28:54 *So that* the man *that is* tender among you, and very delicate, his eye shall be evil toward his brother, and toward the wife of his bosom, and toward the remnant of his children which he shall leave:

28:55 So that he will not give to any of them of the flesh of his children whom he shall eat: because he hath nothing left him in the siege, and in the straitness, wherewith thine enemies shall distress thee in all thy gates.

28:56 The tender and delicate woman among you, which would not adventure to set the sole of her foot upon the ground for delicateness and tenderness, her eye shall be evil toward the husband of her bosom, and toward her son, and toward her daughter,

28:57 And toward her young one that cometh out from between her feet, and toward her children which she shall bear: for she shall eat them for want of all *things* secretly in the siege and straitness, wherewith thine enemy shall distress thee in thy gates.

28:58 If thou wilt not observe to do all the words of this law that are written in this book, that thou mayest fear this glorious and fearful name, THE LORD THY GOD;

28:59 Then the LORD will make thy plagues wonderful, and the plagues of thy seed, *even* great plagues, and of long continuance, and sore sicknesses, and of long continuance.

28:60 Moreover he will bring upon thee all the diseases of Egypt, which thou wast afraid of; and they shall cleave unto thee.

28:61 Also every sickness, and every plague, which *is* not written in the book of this law, them will the LORD bring upon thee, until thou be destroyed.

28:62 And ye shall be left few in number, whereas ye were as the stars of heaven for multitude; because thou wouldest not obey the voice of the LORD thy God.

28:63 And it shall come to pass, *that* as the L<small>ORD</small> rejoiced over you to do you good, and to multiply you; so the L<small>ORD</small> will rejoice over you to destroy you, and to bring you to nought; and ye shall be plucked from off the land whither thou goest to possess it.

28:64 And the L<small>ORD</small> shall scatter thee among all people, from the one end of the earth even unto the other; and there thou shalt serve other gods, which neither thou nor thy fathers have known, *even* wood and stone.

28:65 And among these nations shalt thou find no ease, neither shall the sole of thy foot have rest: but the L<small>ORD</small> shall give thee there a trembling heart, and failing of eyes, and sorrow of mind:

28:66 And thy life shall hang in doubt before thee; and thou shalt fear day and night, and shalt have none assurance of thy life:

28:67 In the morning thou shalt say, Would God it were even! and at even thou shalt say, Would God it were morning! for the fear of thine heart wherewith thou shalt fear, and for the sight of thine eyes which thou shalt see.

28:68 And the L<small>ORD</small> shall bring thee into Egypt again with ships, by the way whereof I spake unto thee, Thou shalt see it no more again: and there ye shall be sold unto your enemies for bondmen and bondwomen, and no man shall buy *you*.

In Christ

Rom 3:24   Being justified freely by his grace through the redemption that is **in Christ** Jesus:

Rom 8:1   *There is* therefore now no condemnation to them which are **in Christ** Jesus, who walk not after the flesh, but after the Spirit.

Rom 8:2   For the law of the Spirit of life **in Christ** Jesus hath made me free from the law of sin and death.

Rom 12:5   So we, *being* many, are one body **in Christ**, and every one members one of another.

1 Cor 1:2   Unto the church of God which is at Corinth, to them that are sanctified **in Christ** Jesus, called *to be* saints, with all that in every place call **upon the name of Jesus Christ** our Lord, both theirs and ours:

1 Cor 1:30   But **of him** are ye **in Christ** Jesus, who of God is made unto us wisdom, and

righteousness, and sanctification, and redemption

1 Cor 15:22   For as in Adam all die, even so **in Christ** shall all be made alive.

2 Cor 2:14   Now thanks *be* unto God, which always causeth us to triumph **in Christ**, and maketh manifest the saviour of his knowledge by us in every place.

2 Cor 3:14   But their minds were blinded: for until this day remaineth the same vail untaken away in the reading of the old testament; which *vail* is done away **in Christ**.

2 Cor 5:17   Therefore if any man *be* **in Christ**, *he is* a new creature: old things are passed away; behold, all things are become new.

2 Cor 5:19   To wit, that God was **in Christ**, reconciling the world unto himself, not imputing their trespasses unto them; and hath committed unto us the word of reconciliation.

Gal 2:4   And that because of false brethren unawares brought in, who came in privily to spy out our liberty which we have **in Christ** Jesus, that they might bring us into bondage:

Gal 3:26	For ye are all the children of God by faith **in Christ** Jesus.
Gal 3:28	There is neither Jew nor Greek, there is neither bond nor free, there is neither male nor female: for ye are all one **in Christ** Jesus.
Gal 5:6	For **in Jesus Christ** neither circumcision availeth any thing, nor uncircumcision; but faith which worketh by love.
Gal 6:15	For **in Christ** Jesus neither circumcision availeth any thing, nor uncircumcision, but a new creature.
Eph 1:3	Blessed *be* the God and Father of our Lord Jesus Christ, who hath blessed us with all spiritual blessings in heavenly *places* **in Christ**:
Eph 1:10	That in the dispensation of the fulness of times he might gather together in one all things **in Christ**, both which are in heaven, and which are on earth; *even* **in him**:
Eph 2:6	And hath raised *us* up together, and made *us* sit together in heavenly *places* **in Christ** Jesus:
Eph 2:10	For we are his workmanship, created **in Christ** Jesus unto good works, which God

hath before ordained that we should walk in them.

Eph 2:13   But now **in Christ** Jesus ye who sometimes were far off are made nigh by the blood **of Christ**.

Eph 3:6   That the Gentiles should be fellowheirs, and of the same body, and partakers of his promise **in Christ** by the gospel:

Phil 3:13-14   Brethren, I count not myself to have apprehended: but *this* one thing *I do*, forgetting those things which are behind, and reaching forth unto those things which are before, I press toward the mark for the prize of the high calling of God **in Christ** Jesus.

1 Th 4:16   For the Lord himself shall descend from heaven with a shout, with the voice of the archangel, and with the trump of God: and the dead **in Christ** shall rise first:

1 Th 5:18   In every thing give thanks: for this is the will of God **in Christ** Jesus concerning you.

1 Tim 1:14   And the grace of our Lord was exceeding abundant with faith and love which is **in Christ** Jesus.

2 Tim 1:9   Who hath saved *us*, and called us with an holy calling, not according to our works, but according to his own purpose and grace, which was given us **in Christ** Jesus before the world began,

2 Tim 1:13   Hold fast the form of sound words, which thou hast heard of me, in faith and love which is **in Christ** Jesus.

2 Tim 2:1   Thou therefore, my son, be strong in the grace that is **in Christ** Jesus.

2 Tim 2:10   Therefore I endure all things for the elect's sakes, that they may also obtain the salvation which is **in Christ** Jesus with eternal glory.

2 Tim 3:15   And that from a child thou hast known the holy scriptures, which are able to make thee wise unto salvation through faith which is **in Christ** Jesus.

Phile 1:6   That the communication of thy faith may become effectual by the acknowledging of every good thing which is in you **in Christ** Jesus.

2 Pet 1:8   For if these things be in you, and abound, they make *you that ye shall* neither *be* barren

nor unfruitful **in** the knowledge of our Lord Jesus **Christ**.

2 Jn 1:9   Whosoever transgresseth, and abideth not **in** the doctrine of **Christ**, hath not God. He that abideth **in** the doctrine of **Christ**, he hath both the Father and the Son.

In Him

Act 17:28   For **in him** we live, and move, and have our being; as certain also of your own poets have said, For we are also his offspring.

Jn 1:4   **In him** was life; and the life was the light of men.

Jn 3:15-16   That whosoever believeth **in him** should not perish, but have eternal life. For God so loved the world, that he gave his only begotten Son, that whosoever believeth **in him** should not perish, but have everlasting life.

2 Cor 1:20   For all the promises of God **in him** *are* yea, and **in him** Amen, unto the glory of God by us.

2 Cor 5:21   For he hath made him *to be* sin for us, who knew no sin; that we might be made the righteousness of God **in him**.

Eph 1:4	According as he hath chosen us **in him** before the foundation of the world, that we should be holy and without blame before him in love:
Eph 1:10	That in the dispensation of the fulness of times he might gather together in one all things **in Christ**, both which are in heaven, and which are on earth; even **in him**:
Phil 3:9	And be found **in him**, not having mine own righteousness, which is of the law, but that which is through the faith **of Christ**, the righteousness which is of God by faith:
Col 2:6	As ye have therefore received Christ Jesus the Lord, *so* walk ye **in him**:
Col 2:7	Rooted and built up **in him**, and stablished in the faith, as ye have been taught, abounding therein with thanksgiving.
Col 2:9	For **in him** dwelleth all the fulness of the Godhead bodily.
Col 2:10	And ye are complete **in him**, which is the head of all principality and power:

1 Jn 2:5   But whoso keepeth his word, **in him** verily is the love of God perfected: hereby know we that we are **in him**.

1 Jn 2:6   He that saith he abideth **in him** ought himself also so to walk, even as he walked.

1 Jn 2:8   Again, a new commandment I write unto you, which thing is true **in him** and in you: because the darkness is past, and the true light now shineth.

1 Jn 2:27   But the anointing which ye have received **of him** abideth in you, and ye need not that any man teach you: but as the same anointing teacheth you of all things, and is truth, and is no lie, and even as it hath taught you, ye shall abide **in him**.

1 Jn 2:28   And now, little children, abide **in him**; that, when he shall appear, we may have confidence, and not be ashamed before him at his coming.

1 Jn 3:3   And every man that hath this hope **in him** purifieth himself, even as he is pure.

1 Jn 3:5   And ye know that he was manifested to take away our sins; and **in him** is no sin.

1 Jn 3:6   Whosoever abideth **in him** sinneth not: whosoever sinneth hath not seen him, neither known him.

1 Jn 3:24   And he that keepeth his commandments dwelleth **in him**, and he **in him**. And hereby we know that he abideth in us, by the Spirit which he hath given us.

1 Jn 4:13   Hereby know we that we dwell **in him**, and he in us, because he hath given us of his Spirit.

1 Jn 4:15   And we have seen and do testify that the Father sent the Son *to be* the Saviour of the world. Whosoever shall confess that Jesus is the Son of God, God dwelleth **in him**, and he in God.

1 Jn 5:20   And we know that the Son of God is come, and hath given us an understanding, that we may know him that is true, and we are **in him** that is true, even in his Son Jesus Christ. This is the true God, and eternal life.

In the Beloved

Eph 1:6   To the praise of the glory of his grace, wherein he hath made us accepted **in the beloved**.

In the Lord

Eph 5:19   Speaking to yourselves in psalms and hymns and spiritual songs, singing and making melody **in** your heart to **the Lord**;

Eph 6:10   Finally, my brethren, be strong **in the Lord**, and in the power of his might.

In Whom

Eph 1:7   **In whom** we have redemption through his blood, the forgiveness of sins, according to the riches of his grace;

Eph 1:11   **In whom** also we have obtained an inheritance, being predestinated according to the purpose **of him** who worketh all things after the counsel of his own will:

Eph 1:13   **In whom** ye also *trusted*, after that ye heard the word of truth, the gospel of your salvation: **in whom** also after that ye believed, ye were sealed with that holy Spirit of promise,

Eph 2:21   **In whom** all the building fitly framed together groweth unto an holy temple **in the Lord**:

Eph 2:22   **In whom** ye also are builded together for
an habitation of God through the Spirit.

Eph 3:12   **In whom** we have boldness and access with
confidence by the faith **of him**.

By Christ

Rom 3:22   Even the righteousness of God *which
is* **by** faith of Jesus **Christ** unto all and
upon all them that believe: for there is
no difference:

Rom 5:15   But not as the offence, so also *is* the free
gift. For if through the offence of one many
be dead, much more the grace of God, and
the gift by grace, *which is* **by** one man, Jesus
Christ, hath abounded unto many.

Rom 5:17-19   For if by one man's offence death reigned
by one; much more they which receive
abundance of grace and of the gift of
righteousness shall reign in life **by**
one, Jesus **Christ**.) Therefore as by the
offence of one *judgment came* upon all
men to condemnation; even so by the
righteousness of one *the free gift came* upon
all men unto justification of life. For as by
one man's disobedience many were made

sinners, so by the obedience of one shall many be made righteous.

Rom 7:4   Wherefore, my brethren, ye also are become dead to the law **by** the body of **Christ**; that ye should be married to another, *even* to him who is raised from the dead, that we should bring forth fruit unto God.

1 Cor 1:4   I thank my God always on your behalf, for the grace of God which is given you **by** Jesus **Christ**

2 Cor 5:18   And all things *are* of God, who hath reconciled us to himself **by** Jesus **Christ**, and hath given to us the ministry of reconciliation;

Gal 2:16   Knowing that a man is not justified by the works of the law, but **by** the faith of Jesus **Christ**, even we have believed in Jesus Christ, that we might be justified **by** the faith of **Christ**, and not by the works of the law: for by the works of the law shall no flesh be justified.

Eph 1:5   Having predestinated us unto the adoption of children **by** Jesus **Christ** to himself, according to the good pleasure of his will,

Phil 1:11   Being filled with the fruits of righteousness, which are **by** Jesus **Christ**, unto the glory and praise of God.

Phil 4:19   But my God shall supply all your need according to his riches in glory **by Christ** Jesus.

1 Pet 1:3   Blessed *be* the God and Father of our Lord Jesus Christ, which according to his abundant mercy hath begotten us again unto a lively hope **by** the resurrection of Jesus **Christ** from the dead,

1 Pet 2:5   Ye also, as lively stones, are built up a spiritual house, an holy priesthood, to offer up spiritual sacrifices, acceptable to God **by** Jesus **Christ**.

1 Pet 5:10   But the God of all grace, who hath called us unto his eternal glory **by Christ** Jesus, after that ye have suffered a while, make you perfect, stablish, strengthen, settle *you*.

By Him

1 Cor 1:5   That in every thing ye are enriched **by him**, *in* all utterance, and in all knowledge;

1 Cor 8:6   But to us *there is but* one God, the Father, of whom *are* all things, and we **in him**; and

one Lord Jesus Christ, **by whom** *are* all things, and we **by him**.

Col 1:16 For **by him** were all things created, that are in heaven, and that are in earth, visible and invisible, whether *they be* thrones, or dominions, or principalities, or powers: all things were created **by him**, and for him:

Col 1:17 And he is before all things, and **by him** all things consist.

Col 1:20 And, having made peace through the blood of his cross, **by him** to reconcile all things unto himself; **by him**, *I say*, whether *they be* things in earth, or things in heaven.

Col 3:17 And whatsoever ye do in word or deed, *do* all in the name of the Lord Jesus, giving thanks to God and the Father **by him**.

Heb 7:25 Wherefore he is able also to save them to the uttermost that come unto God **by him**, seeing he ever liveth to make intercession for them.

Heb 13:15 **By him** therefore let us offer the sacrifice of praise to God continually, that is, the fruit of *our* lips giving thanks to his name.

1 Pet 1:21   Who **by him** do believe in God, that raised him up from the dead, and gave him glory; that your faith and hope might be in God.

By Himself

Heb 1:3   Who being the brightness of *his* glory, and the express image of his person, and upholding all things by the word of his power, when he had **by himself** purged our sins, sat down on the right hand of the Majesty on high;

Heb 9:26   For then must he often have suffered since the foundation of the world: but now once in the end of the world hath he appeared to put away sin **by** the sacrifice of **himself**.

By His Blood

Heb 9:11-12   But Christ being come an high priest of good things to come, by a greater and more perfect tabernacle, not made with hands, that is to say, not of this building; Neither by the blood of goats and calves, but **by his own blood** he entered in once into the holy place, having obtained eternal redemption *for us*.

Heb 9:14-15   How much more shall **the blood of Christ**, who through the eternal Spirit offered himself without spot to God, purge your conscience from dead works to serve the living God? And for this cause he is the mediator of the new testament, that by means of death, for the redemption of the transgressions *that were* under the first testament, they which are called might receive the promise of eternal inheritance.

Heb 10:19-20   Having therefore, brethren, boldness to enter into the holiest **by the blood of Jesus,** By a new and living way, which he hath consecrated for us, through the veil, that is to say, his flesh;

1 Jn 1:7   But if we walk in the light, as he is in the light, we have fellowship one with another, and **the blood of Jesus Christ** his Son cleanseth us from all sin.

By Whom

Rom 5:2   **By whom** also we have access by faith into this grace wherein we stand, and rejoice in hope of the glory of God.

Rom 5:11   And not only *so*, but we also joy in God through our Lord Jesus Christ, **by whom** we have now received the atonement.

Gal 6:14   But God forbid that I should glory, save in the cross of our Lord Jesus Christ, **by whom** the world is crucified unto me, and I unto the world.

From Whom

Eph 4:16   **From whom** the whole body fitly joined together and compacted by that which every joint supplieth, according to the effectual working in the measure of every part, maketh increase of the body unto the edifying of itself in love.

Of Christ

2 Cor 1:5   For as the sufferings **of Christ** abound in us, so our consolation also aboundeth **by Christ**.

Phil 3:12   Not as though I had already attained, either were already perfect: but I follow after, if that I may apprehend that for which also I am apprehended **of Christ** Jesus.

Col 2:17   Which are a shadow of things to come; but the body *is* **of Christ**.

Col 3:24   Knowing that **of the Lord** ye shall receive
the reward of the inheritance: for ye serve
the Lord Christ.

Of Him

1 Jn 1:5   This then is the message which we have
heard **of him**, and declare unto you, that
God is light, and **in him** is no darkness at all.

1 Jn 2:27   But the anointing which ye have received
of him abideth in you, and ye need not
that any man teach you: but as the same
anointing teacheth you of all things, and
is truth, and is no lie, and even as it hath
taught you, ye shall abide **in him**.

Through Christ

Rom 5:1   Therefore being justified by faith, we have
peace with God **through** our Lord Jesus **Christ**:

Rom 5:11   And not only *so*, but we also joy in God
through our Lord Jesus **Christ, by whom**
we have now received the atonement.

Rom 6:11   Likewise reckon ye also yourselves to be
dead indeed unto sin, but alive unto God
through Jesus **Christ** our Lord.

Rom 6:23   For the wages of sin *is* death; but the gift of God *is* eternal life **through** Jesus **Christ** our Lord.

1 Cor 15:57   But thanks *be* to God, which giveth us the victory **through** our Lord Jesus **Christ**.

Gal 3:13-14   Christ hath redeemed us from the curse of the law, being made a curse for us: for it is written, Cursed *is* every one that hangeth on a tree: That the blessing of Abraham might come on the Gentiles **through** Jesus **Christ**; that we might receive the promise of the Spirit through faith.

Gal 4:7   Wherefore thou art no more a servant, but a son; and if a son, then an heir of God **through Christ**.

Eph 2:7   That in the ages to come he might shew the exceeding riches of his grace in his kindness toward us **through Christ** Jesus.

Phil 4:7   And the peace of God, which passeth all understanding, shall keep your hearts and minds **through Christ** Jesus.

Phil 4:13   I can do all things **through Christ** which strengtheneth me.

Heb 10:10   By the which will we are sanctified **through** the offering of the body of Jesus **Christ** once *for all.*

Heb 13:20-21 Now the God of peace, that brought again from the dead our Lord Jesus, that great shepherd of the sheep, through the blood of the everlasting covenant, Make you perfect in every good work to do his will, working in you that which is wellpleasing in his sight, **through** Jesus **Christ;** to whom *be* glory for ever and ever. Amen.

Through Him

Jn 1:7   The same came for a witness, to bear witness of the Light, that all *men* **through him** might believe.

Jn 3:17   For God sent not his Son into the world to condemn the world; but that the world **through him** might be saved.

Rom 5:9   Much more then, being now justified by his blood, we shall be saved from wrath **through him.**

Rom 8:37   Nay, in all these things we are more than conquerors **through him** that loved us.

1 Jn 4:9   In this was manifested the love of God toward us, because that God sent his only begotten Son into the world, that we might live **through him**.

With Christ

Rom 6:8   Now if we be dead **with Christ**, we believe that we shall also live **with him**:

Gal 2:20   I am crucified **with Christ**: nevertheless I live; yet not I, but Christ liveth in me: and the life which I now live in the flesh I live by the faith of the Son of God, who loved me, and gave himself for me.

Eph 2:5   Even when we were dead in sins, hath quickened us together **with Christ**, (by grace ye are saved;)

Col 2:20   Wherefore if ye be dead **with Christ** from the rudiments of the world, why, as though living in the world, are ye subject to ordinances,

Col 3:1   If ye then be risen **with Christ**, seek those things which are above, where Christ sitteth on the right hand of God.

Col 3:3   For ye are dead, and your life is hid **with Christ** in God.

With Him

Rom 6:4   Therefore we are buried **with him** by baptism into death: that like as Christ was raised up from the dead by the glory of the Father, even şo we also should walk in newness of life.

Rom 6:6   Knowing this, that our old man is crucified **with him**, that the body of sin might be destroyed, that henceforth we should not serve sin.

Rom 6:8   Now if we be dead **with Christ**, we believe that we shall also live **with him**:

Rom 8:32   He that spared not his own Son, but delivered him up for us all, how shall he not **with him** also freely give us all things?

2 Cor 13:4   For though he was crucified through weakness, yet he liveth by the power of God. For we also are weak **in him**, but we shall live **with him** by the power of God toward you.

Col 2:12-15   Buried **with him** in baptism, wherein also
ye are risen **with him** through the faith
of the operation of God, who hath raised
him from the dead. And you, being dead
in your sins and the uncircumcision of
your flesh, hath he quickened together
with him, having forgiven you all
trespasses; Blotting out the handwriting
of ordinances that was against us, which
was contrary to us, and took it out of the
way, nailing it to his cross; *And* having
spoiled principalities and powers, he
made a shew of them openly, triumphing
over them in it.

Col 3:4   When Christ, *who is* our life, shall
appear, then shall ye also appear **with
him** in glory.

2 Tim 2:11-12 *It is* a faithful saying: For if we be dead
with him, we shall also live **with him**: If we
suffer, we shall also reign **with him**: if we
deny *him*, he also will deny us:

By Me

Jn 6:57   As the living Father hath sent me, and I live
by the Father: so he that eateth me, even he
shall live **by me**.

Jn 14:6	Jesus saith unto him, I am the way, the truth, and the life: no man cometh unto the Father, but **by me**.

In Me

Jn 6:56	He that eateth my flesh, and drinketh my blood, dwelleth **in me**, and I **in him**.
Jn 14:20	At that day ye shall know that I *am* in my Father, and ye **in me**, and I in you.
Jn 15:4-5	Abide **in me**, and I in you. As the branch cannot bear fruit of itself, except it abide in the vine; no more can ye, except ye abide **in me**. I am the vine, ye *are* the branches: He that abideth **in me**, and I in him, the same bringeth forth much fruit: for without me ye can do nothing.
Jn 15:7-8	If ye abide **in me**, and my words abide in you, ye shall ask what ye will, and it shall be done unto you. Herein is my Father glorified, that ye bear much fruit; so shall ye be my disciples.
Jn 16:33	These things I have spoken unto you, that **in me** ye might have peace. In the world ye

shall have tribulation: but be of good cheer;
I have overcome the world.

In My Love

Jn 15:9   As the Father hath loved me, so have I
loved you: continue ye **in my love**.

In My Name

Mt 18:20   For where two or three are gathered
together **in my name**, there am I in the
midst of them.

Mar 16:17   And these signs shall follow them that
believe; **In my name** shall they cast out
devils; they shall speak with new tongues;

Jn 14:13-14   And whatsoever ye shall ask **in my name**,
that will I do, that the Father may be
glorified in the Son. If ye shall ask any thing
in my name, I will do *it*.

Jn 16:23-24   And in that day ye shall ask me nothing.
Verily, verily, I say unto you, Whatsoever
ye shall ask the Father **in my name**, he will
give *it* you. Hitherto have ye asked nothing
in my name: ask, and ye shall receive, that
your joy may be full.

End Notes

Chapter One

[1] Mackintosh, C. H. (1862). *Notes on Exodus*. (3rd ed.). Stem Publishing: Ramsgate, Kent, UK. <http://www.amcbryan.binternet.co.uk/docs.htm >.

[2] Mackintosh, *Notes on Exodus*.

Chapter Two

[1] Blue Letter Bible. "Dictionary and Word Search for *'poterion (Strong's 4221) ' "*. Blue Letter Bible. 1996-2002. <http://www.blueletterbible.org>.

[2] Dake's Annotated Reference Bible. (large print ed.). (2002). *6 Things Christians Should Not Suffer*. Dake Publishing, Inc. Lawrenceville, Georgia. p. 897 in the O.T.

[3] Dake's, *Of What Christian Suffering Consists Of*. p. 473 in the N.T.

[4] Noah Webster's First Edition of An American Dictionary of the English Language. (1828). *"Sovereign."* Foundation for American Christian Education: San Francisco, California. (15th reprint, 2002).

[5] Liardon, R. (Ed.) (1999). *John G. Lake, The Complete Collection Of His Life Teachings*. Albury Publishing, Tulsa, Oklahoma. p. 780.

[6] Mackintosh, *Notes on Exodus.*

[7] Mackintosh, *Notes on Exodus.*

[8] Mackintosh, *Notes on Exodus.*

[9] Mackintosh, *Notes on Exodus.*

Chapter Three

[1] Blue Letter Bible. *"nacag (Strong's 05254)."*

[2] Mackintosh, *Notes on Exodus.*

[3] Mackintosh, *Notes on Exodus.*

[4] Mackintosh, *Notes on Exodus.*

[5] Mackintosh, *Notes on Exodus.*

Chapter Four

[1] Blue Letter Bible. *"peirasmos (Strong's 3986)."*

[2] Blue Letter Bible. *"nacag (Strong's 05254)."*

[3] Webster's First Edition, *"Tempt."*

[4] Mackintosh, *Notes on Exodus.*

[5] Mackintosh, *Notes on Exodus.*

Chapter 5

[1] Dake's, p. 897 in the O.T.

2 Dake's, p. 473 in the N.T.

3 Blue Letter Bible. *"martus (Strong's 3144)."*

4 Church, L. F. (Ed.) *Matthew Henry's Commentary.* (1961). Zondervan: Grand Rapids, MI. p. 1343.

5 Mackintosh, *Notes on Exodus.*

6 Mackintosh, *Notes on Exodus.*

7 Mackintosh, *Notes on Exodus.*

8 Mackintosh, *Notes on Exodus.*

9 Mackintosh, *Notes on Exodus.*

10 Mackintosh, *Notes on Exodus.*

11 Mackintosh, *Notes on Exodus.*

12 Mackintosh, *Notes on Exodus.*

13 Mackintosh, *Notes on Exodus.*

Chapter Six

1 Church, p. 1214.

2 Church, p. 9.

3 Church, p. 1215.

4 Blue Letter Bible. *"eremia (Strong's 2047)."*

5 Blue Letter Bible, *"eremos (Strong's 2048). "*

6 Dake's, p. 897 in the O.T.

7 Mackintosh, *Notes on Exodus.*

8 Mackintosh, *Notes on Exodus.*

9 Mackintosh, *Notes on Deuteronomy.*

10 Mackintosh, *Notes on Deuteronomy.*

Chapter Seven

1 Dake's, Note m, 3rd Column, p. 35 in the O.T.

2 Blue Letter Bible. *"charis (Strong's 5485)."*

3 Blue Letter Bible. *"dikaios (Strong's 13432)."*

4 Dake's, p. 355 in the N.T.

5 Dake's, p. 356 in the N.T.

6 Dake's, p. 356 in the N.T.

7 Dake's, p. 356 in the N.T.

8 Dake's, p. 357 in the N.T.

9 Dake's, p. 357 in the N.T.

10 Dake's, p. 357 in the N.T.

Bibliography

Blue Letter Bible. (1996-2002). <http://www.blueletter bible.org>.

Church, L. F. (Ed.) *Matthew Henry's Commentary.* (1961). Zondervan: Grand Rapids, MI.

Dake's Annotated Reference Bible. (large print ed.). (2002). Dake Publishing, Inc. Lawrenceville, Georgia.

Liardon, R. (Ed.) (1999). *Lake, John G. The Complete Collection Of His Life Teachings.* Albury Publishing, Tulsa, Oklahoma.

Mackintosh, C. H. (1862). *Notes on Exodus.* (3rd ed.). Stem Publishing: Ramsgate, Kent, UK. <http://www. amcbryan.binternet.co.uk/docs.htm>.

Mackintosh, C. H. *Notes on Deuteronomy.* Stem Publishing: Ramsgate, Kent, UK. <http://www. amcbryan.binternet.co.uk/docs.htm>.

Noah Webster's First Edition of An American Dictionary of the English Language. (1828). Foundation for American Christian Education: San Francisco, California. (15th reprint, 2002).

ORDER FORM

Quantity	Title	Sug. Don.	Total
	My Sheep Will Know My Voice	$ 10.00	
	My Sheep Will Know My Voice (Study Guide)	$ 2.00	
	Will the Real God Please Stand Up	$15.00	

Shipping Charges		
$ 0.01 - $ 10.99	$ 2.00
$ 11.00 - $ 49.99	$ 3.00
$ 50.00 - $ 99.99	$ 4.00
$100.00 - $ 199.99	$ 6.00
$200.00 -	$ 8.00

Subtotal

Shipping and handling

Enclosed is my seed faith gift

Total

Make check or money order payable to:
Rejoyce Moore Ministries, Inc.

Mail to:
**Robin Moore Joyce
Rejoyce Moore Ministries, Inc.
428 Cokain Road
Harrisville, PA 16038**

For more information, we may be reached at:
814-758-2263 or **814-786-9358**
www.rejoycemoore.com